SOLUTION-ORIENTED HYPNOSIS

An Ericksonian Approach

SOLUTION-ORIENTED HYPNOSIS

An Ericksonian Approach

William Hudson O'Hanlon

Michael Martin

W. W. Norton & Company, Inc. · New York · London

Printed in the United States of America.

First Edition

The text of this book was composed in Sabon.
Composition by Bytheway Typesetting Services, Inc.
Manufacturing by Haddon Craftsmen, Inc.
Book design by Justine Burkat Trubey

Library of Congress Cataloging-in-Publication Data

O'Hanlon, William Hudson.
 Solution-oriented hypnosis : an Ericksonian approach / William
Hudson O'Hanlon, Michael Martin.
     p.   cm.
 "A Norton professional Book."
 Includes bibliographical references.
 ISBN 0-393-70149-2
 1. Hypnotism — Therapeutic use.   2. Erickson, Milton H.
I. Martin, Michael, 1951– . II. Title.
 [DNLM: 1. Hypnosis — methods.   WM 415 036s]
RC495.034 1992
615.8′512 — dc20
DNLM/DLC   92-16410 CIP
for Library of Congress

W.W. Norton & Company, Inc., 500 Fifth Avenue, New York, N.Y. 10110
W.W. Norton & Company, Ltd., 10 Coptic Street, London WC1A 1PU

6 7 8 9 0

To Pat and Patrick, who have entranced me since I've known them. And to R. Lofton Hudson, my father-in-law, who is an excellent hypnotist despite the fact he probably agrees with very little in this book. — W. H. O.

To Betsy and Becca. — M. M.

CONTENTS

ACKNOWLEDGMENTS

THANKS TO SANDY KUTLER, Gail Hartman, Mary Neuman, and Pat Hudson for their proofreading and suggestions. (They all learned that I'm very suggestible.) Thanks to Bonnie Ferus for all the typing. Thanks to Margaret Farley at Norton for staying awake while editing the inductions. As always, thanks to Susan Barrows Munro for supporting me in following my bliss (and indulging my choice for the cover art). And thanks to Michael for keeping the project alive and moving. — W. H. O.

PREFACE

THIS BOOK WAS RECORDED AT A workshop I presented on Hilton Head, South Carolina in December, 1989. Michael Martin, my best friend, recorded it and transcribed it. He also did the initial editing.

I am excited about it because it is the first of my books that I think captures the energy, irreverence, humor, and clarity of my teaching. I like to teach much more than I like to write (although I do love to have written), and I've been consistently frustrated that I haven't been able yet to write in the lively manner that I teach. So, finally, here is a fairly good representation of what I do in workshops captured on the printed page. I say fairly good, because you really have to be there to get all the nonverbals, which are half the show. But this is the next best thing to being there.

—Bill O'Hanlon
January, 1992

SOLUTION-ORIENTED HYPNOSIS

An Ericksonian Approach

ONE

The Elements of Solution-Oriented Hypnosis

Introinduction

I'm Bill O'Hanlon. This is a workshop on solution-oriented hypnosis. We have two days to bring you, if you haven't had any background in hypnosis at all, from not knowing anything about it, from maybe thinking hypnosis is like voodoo, to competency in doing solution-oriented hypnosis.

I have an outrageous promise to make to you. By the end of this workshop, by the end of the two days, if you participate in the exercises, you'll be able to induce a trance. Some of you are probably thinking, "Oh, I don't know about this stuff. I don't even know if I believe in hypnosis," so that's a bit of a leap for you. But I've done the workshop enough times so I can promise that much, even if you're a complete novice and skeptic.

Some of you have already had a fair amount of background in hypnosis, and what I intend this workshop to be for you is a clarification. I used to be a workshop junkie, and I went to a lot of workshops. After a while I got kind of disgusted because I'd go to a workshop and someone would spend three days putting me in trance and looking meaningfully into my eyes while they were talking about my conscious mind and my unconscious mind. I'd spend three days in sort of a semi-trance state, and at the end of the three days I'd think, "You know, they keep saying my unconscious is going to learn this, my unconscious is going to learn this." After a while, though, I thought, well, I'd like my **conscious** mind to learn this, because I'm one of these people who like to **know** what I know consciously. So this workshop will probably be different from most of the other Ericksonian workshops you've been to, if you've been to any of them. That is, it will be a little more explicit. I'm trying to make things as clear and simple as possible. So you can be empowered to not only know about it, but to do it.

Because I've taught a lot of workshops and sat through a lot of workshops, I've learned a few things about doing them. One of the things I've learned is that people seem to learn in different ways. And so I've tried to make this workshop as multimodal as possible, as multimedia as possible. I'll be writing some things on the board, I'll be showing some videotapes, I'll be playing some audiotapes. You'll have some handouts that will summarize the didactic material. So, if you don't like to take notes, you don't have to take notes. You're welcome to take notes, though, if you want. But the handouts will summarize the main points. And, I'll have you do some practice exercises. I'll do some live demonstrations. I've read enough feedback forms to know that if I leave out one learning modality, people write, "Wish we could have had some live demos," "Wish we could have had some videotapes," "Wish we could have had more practice," or "Wanted handouts to summarize materials."

So here you'll have all the modalities. By teaching you the elements of solution-oriented hypnosis and having you practice it a little piece at a time, we're going to walk you up to competency in induction. That will be it for the first day, which will focus on induction.

On the second day we will get to the question, which for me is the $64,000 question when I learned hypnosis: "Well, what do I do once they get into trance?" In the Ericksonian tradition, there's this idea of "trusting the unconscious," so do I just let them hang out in trance and trust their unconscious to solve their problem? Or am I actually supposed to do something once they get into trance? Tomorrow will give the answer — *my* answer — to that question. What to do once they get into trance. And I think it involves more than just letting them hang out and letting their creative unconscious do it; more than just reprogramming them with positive beliefs.

Tomorrow we'll also talk about **when** you would ever use hypnosis, because you might have gotten along in your clinical practice just fine so far without ever using hypnosis. And, secondly, **what** to do once people get into trance.

Today's question is: How do you induce a trance with just about everybody?

Traditional vs. Ericksonian Approaches to Induction

Let me first contrast traditional approaches to hypnosis, which are typically more authoritarian, and Ericksonian or permissive approaches (which aren't always strictly equal, but close enough for our purposes today).

Traditional approaches say there are some people you can induce a trance with and some people you can't. Some people are hypnotizable and suggestible, some people aren't. But for clinical purposes, when we want to use trance, we're going to have to be able to use it with a wide range of people. Even those who are not classically hypnotizable or suggestible.

An Ericksonian approach says that you can do trance with just about everybody. Everybody is hypnotizable. You've just got to find the ways in which they're responsive and hypnotizable.

In traditional approaches, you know, the stuff you see in movies or on stage, or that you read in books or whatever, it's the hypnotist with the magnetic personality and eyes who says: "You **vill** go into trance and you **vill** obey me." "Yes, Master" and a zombified appearance is the expected response. And, in traditional approaches, even though it's not as dramatic as the movies or Svengali, there is still an element of that. The person who is doing the induction is supposed to run the show and to tell the person what it is they **will** experience and **are** experiencing.

Traditional hypnotists typically use words that are predictive or attributional. They attribute feelings or thoughts or experiences or actions to people. If I say, "Your eyes will close, your eyes are getting heavier and heavier and you'll become very, very relaxed," or "You are becoming very, very relaxed, you are going deeper and deeper into a trance, you will go deeper and deeper into a trance." I'm telling you what **will** happen or what **is** happening. And either in your behavior or your experience, I'm supposed to be able to tell you what happens and then have it happen.

This works well for those 25% of people who are highly hypnotizable and very suggestible. You say, "Your eyes will close," and — boom — their eyes close and everything is hunky-dory. There are about 50% of people who are **somewhat** hypnotizable and **somewhat** suggestible, and with those people, they will respond depending on the conditions and depending on your skills. And 25% of people **aren't** hypnotizable, **aren't** suggestible in the traditional hypnosis scheme of things. So these approaches will typically do really well with the first 25%. When you say "Your eyelids are feeling heavier and heavier," their eyelids will start to feel heavier. When you say, "You'll go deeper into trance," they'll start to go deeper into trance. Everything is hunky-dory.

The problem is the last 25% who don't respond to those traditional approaches. Things aren't so hunky-dory there. If I say to them, "Your eyelids are getting heavier and heavier" and "Your eyes are starting to close," and their eyes open wider, I'm in deep trouble. Usually what's concluded is either I'm not a good hypnotist or you're not a good subject. Given the nature of our field we usually conclude that they're not a good subject and that they're resistant. That's the face-saving way for us to handle it.

The Utilization Approach

Ericksonian approaches bypass this difficulty in various ways. One of the ways is using **permissive** words. We don't try to force people in any sort of direction or take it on ourselves to **make** them do things or to open up the possibility of failure. We use permissive words like "you could," "you can," and "you might." Instead of saying "Your eyes **will** close or **are** closing," you say, "Your eyes **could** close" or "You **might** want to close your eyes, I don't really know." So we use more empowering words, permissive words. This approach bypasses that struggle for control that people sometimes have. Almost everybody doesn't want to be controlled by someone else, whether they're clients or just the general public. That's their fear, that somebody's going to control them and they fear that hypnosis is one of the ways that someone could control them.

The other means of bypassing control and resistance is to give lots of options, lots of possibilities, sort of "multiple choice" options. Let the person decide how it is that they will go into trance. I can say, "You can go into trance with your eyes open or your eyes closed, whatever is more comfortable for you." "Would you like to go into trance sitting in *that* chair or would you like to go into trance in another chair?" You give them some choices: "You can go into trance being distracted, listening to everything I say, or you might be drifting off into your own thoughts. You might be very focused on what I'm saying, you might be very focused on what's here in the room, or you might be drifting away someplace else, some other time." Those are all possibilities. So we give lots of choices, instead of saying, "This is the way you **will** do it" or "This is the way you **are** doing it" or "You **have** to do it."

A third way to bypass resistance and create cooperation is to validate whatever response that person gives as appropriate and okay, rather than implying that they have to do it the way you think they should do it. Some people won't come in and do the typical thing of sitting on a chair, putting their hands on their thighs and relaxing. That's not the way they're going to go into trance. In fact, they'll do the exact opposite of that. They'll be very uptight, they won't be relaxed at all.

Erickson had an approach he called the "Utilization Approach." The Utilization Approach is just a fancy name for "Use whatever the person brings into therapy." Whatever they bring to the hypnotic situation, you use. You give them the sense that it's okay to be doing that, and you help them use that in going into trance. Erickson would use people's symptoms as trance inductions or therapeutic techniques. He would use their resistance. He'd use their belief systems or delusions.

I was working with a woman who believed that God was making her grow younger and was going to have her kill herself and go up to Heaven. You have to somehow use those belief systems or you're going to be left behind with that particular person. She believed she was a young child rather than 28 years old. If you come in conflict with those ideas, and you think that they have to have your belief system before they can get psychotherapy, it's going to be tough going.

The Utilization Approach says to use whatever the person brings, in terms of their presenting behavior or whatever it may be. And in hypnosis, use whatever the clients brings to the hypnotic situation as part of the trance induction. I can think of a classic example from Erickson's work:

A guy comes into Erickson's office, begins to speak very rapidly while pacing back and forth, and says, "I suppose you'll throw me out of your office like all the other psychiatrists have, like all the other doctors have, because I can't sit down in a chair, I can't tell you what my problem is, I can't free associate, I can't do any of that stuff, I get very, very uptight before I come to a doctor's office, but as soon as I get into a doctor's office, this is all I can do—I can walk around like this, I can't sit on a chair, I can't tell you what my problem is." So you might say he's a little nervous.

So Erickson says, "Well, would you mind walking back and forth in my office?" And the man says, "Would I mind? Good God, man, I've told you I have to walk back and forth in your office or I can't stay here. No, I wouldn't mind." And Erickson says, "Would you mind, as you're walking back and forth in my office, if I talk to you?" "No, that's why I'm here, for you to talk to me, for me to talk to you, but don't ask me to sit down, don't ask me to tell you what my problem is, I can't tell you what my problem is." And so on. And every once in a while the man takes a breath, and Erickson says something in the interim. One of the first things Erickson says is, "Walk over to this chair. Now turn around, now walk over to this chair. Now turn around, now walk over to this chair. Now walk over to that chair. Now turn around and walk back to that chair. Now turn around and walk to that chair. Now turn around over there and walk to that chair. Now turn back around and walk over to this chair.

Now walk to that chair. Now turn around and walk back to that chair. Now you've gotten there, now turn around, now walk back to that chair. Now you're in the middle. Now turn around and walk to that chair. Now turn around and walk back to the middle, and walk to that chair. Now turn around, and walk to the middle and walk to that chair. Now turn around and walk away from this chair. Now that you've gotten there, now start to turn around, now turn around, now walk over to that chair. Now you're halfway there, now turn to that chair. Walk to that chair."

Erickson just starts directing his walking. And it's okay with the guy, just as long as Erickson doesn't ask him to sit down, doesn't ask him to tell him what his problems are.

Erickson soon starts to change a couple of things. One of the things he starts to change is how quickly he speaks. At first he's speaking very, very rapidly, like the man's speaking and like the man's walking. Erickson then starts to slow down his rate of speaking, just a little. "Now you can walk over to that chair." And the guy starts to, in response, walk a little slower. "Now you've gotten to that chair, now you've turned around, now start to walk toward that chair, now you've gotten in the middle of it, in the middle of the room, now walk over to that chair. [slight pause] Now you've gotten there, now you start to turn around. . . . " And Erickson slows down more and more.

He also does another thing. He stops and takes a breath just before he gives the next instruction to the guy. Now the guy's gotten used to listening to Erickson telling him where to walk, and without the instruction he doesn't know where to walk. So he waits for the next instruction and Erickson takes a nice, deep breath. And the guy hesitates. "Now walk over to that chair. Now you've gotten there, now start to turn around, now turn around, now walk to that chair. Now you've gotten there, now start to turn around. Now turn around. Now walk to that chair. Now you've gotten there. [pause] Now turn around. Now walk over to that chair. Now you've gotten to that chair, now turn around. [pause] And walk towards that chair."

Gradually he starts to introduce smaller pieces, "Now you've gotten halfway there, now you've gotten three-quarters of the way there, now turn around." He gets him to hesitate. When he's three-quarters of the way there he says, "and walk over to the other chair." He starts to break it up piece by piece.

Then Erickson starts to introduce another element. "Now look at each of the chairs, walk to each of the chairs, and look at each of them and figure out which chair you'd be the least uncomfortable sitting in." So the man looks at all the chairs, thinks about it a few times as he's walking back and forth. And he decides that he'd be the least uncomfortable sitting in *that* chair. So Erickson says, "Now walk toward the chair you'd be the least uncomfortable sitting in, now walk away from the chair you'd be the least uncomfortable sitting in. Now walk towards this chair. Now walk toward the chair you'd be the least uncomfortable sitting in, now walk away from the chair you'd be the most comfortable sitting in. Walk towards the chair, walk towards the chair you'd be the most comfortable sitting in. Walk away from the chair you'd be the most comfortable sitting in." So, subtly, he starts to change it from the *least uncomfortable* to the *most comfortable* chair. Gradually, as he's hesitating in front of this chair, wondering when he cold possibly sit down on it, walking away from it, walking towards it, he starts to hesitate in front of it, and starts to sit down and Erickson says, "Don't sit down yet." And he walks away from it and walks towards it, and gradually he starts to sit down on the chair, in which he could be the most comfortable. And as he sits down, Erickson says, "As you sit down all the way in that chair you can go all the way into trance."

Now that's a different kind of trance induction than "You **vill** go into a trance" and "Watch the watch." It's a different kind of trance induction than "You really have to relax and concentrate in order to go into trance." It's a very, very different model. The model is take whatever they're showing you and include it, utilize it as part of the trance induction.

Instead of saying, "You have to come to the model I have of hypnosis," I'd better come to the model of the world you have and meet you there and help lead you into hypnosis. So this explains the outrageous claim of the Ericksonian approach that everyone can be hypnotized. It's just the method of finding how **they** go into trance. That involves utilizing whatever **they** are showing, validating their responses and building up a responsiveness so that you can find out how **this** person's going to go into trance. They can teach you how to induce them into trance.

> I had a ten-year-old kid come for therapy for school phobias and I was doing some hypnosis with him. I used a counting technique (which I rarely use). I was counting down from 20 to one for him to go into a trance. And I'd say "20, now you can start to go into hypnosis, into a trance, 19. . . . " And as I started to talk like that, he started to giggle, he was feeling self-conscious. So he started to giggle. And I said, "I think giggling is a great way to go into trance . . . 18 . . . because so many adults usually are so *serious* about hypnosis. So grim about hypnosis. 17 . . . and I think that giggling your way into trance is a nice way to go into trance . . . 16." And I started to talk like that and when I got to 5 in my counting he had stopped giggling. He just went into a more quiet trance. So we did a bunch of trance work. About 25 minutes later I was starting to have him come out of trance and I started to count up from one to 20. And to his surprise and a bit to my surprise, as soon as I got to 5 he began to giggle again, and he giggled his way out of trance from 5 to 20.

Now that's the giggling technique for going into trance, and that was his technique. It's not my technique and it may not be anybody else's technique. But that's **his** technique. The other guy that we talked about before had the pace-back-and-forth-in-Erickson's-office technique. Whatever particular approach that the client has, it can be utilized by the hypnotist, by the therapist. It needs to be included, one way or another.

People will come in with all sorts of ideas. Some think hypnosis means they have to be controlled by someone else. So what you want to do is include in the circle of trance anything that they think can't be included or might potentially invalidate their trance experience.

If they say, "I can't concentrate," you'd better include that in there and say, "You don't really have to concentrate to go into trance." Whatever their idea is, **include** it. If they indicate that they think trance necessitates paying attention to everything that you say or they'll have to really memorize everything you say, you'd better give them permission not to. "You don't have to memorize everything I say or you don't have to listen." If they say, "I don't think I can go into a trance because I need to be in control," you say, "It's okay to be in control and you could discover that you are in control in ways that you don't even notice, that you might be in unconscious control of things, conscious control of things, but the trance really isn't about one person controlling another person."

Bandler and Grinder used to make this joke: "You ask people what they think trance is and they'll say, 'I won't see anything, I won't feel, I won't hear anything,' and they'd replay, 'Well that's dead, now what do you think trance is?'" That was one way to challenge people's sometimes unrealistic expectations regarding trance. (I used to use that joke until one time I went into a trance where I didn't see anything, didn't feel anything, didn't hear anything. I don't use that joke anymore.) Usually I'll give people a little rap as we start and find out what some of their ideas about trance are or some of their apprehensions, some of their frames of reference. Then I'll either include those and say, "Yes, that could happen in trance," or I'll dismiss them and say, "Well you know, some people have this idea that they'll be knocked out while they're in trance and that's usually not true." You can demystify or gently challenge their ideas about trance. I'll give them a little talk before trance, during trance, or after trance to say "You could include this," whatever they thought they couldn't include and/or "This is not a necessity." Things like "You don't have to concentrate on everything I'm saying. You don't have to listen to everything I'm saying" or "You could listen to everything I'm saying, but you don't have to, you could drift away." Somehow I have to include whatever they are doing or might do. This is my circle of trance and I want to include a bunch of stuff and then also say that they don't have to do certain stuff. Give them permission and validate them for wherever they are and give them the sense that whatever they are doing is okay. It's not a block, whether it's giggling, walking back and forth, not concentrating, or concentrating a lot.

Some people come out of trance and say, "I couldn't have been in trance because I've heard everything you said." So, usually before trance, I'll say something about that, I'll say, "Probably the most surprising thing is you might be able to hear everything that I'm saying when you are in trance." So all of a sudden that includes hearing everything I say when you are in trace, so they won't come out of the trance and say, "I couldn't have been in trace because I heard everything you said." Just give that permission to do whatever they're doing. That's the first thing. Let me give you a handout (1.1) that will summarize some of this stuff. It's called "Elements of Solution-Oriented Induction."

Permission / Validation / Observation / Utilization

The first element is permission, validation, utilization. Utilization means utilizing what people bring to the situation, giving them permission for being whatever they are and then communicating to them that any response they give is okay. Because what we are trying to build up here is a good context, a nice context that facilitates trance and that empowers people, and also a sense of responsiveness. I'm going to find out what it is that you are going to respond to. I'm going to be talking to you about various things, doing various behaviors around you, and I'm going to see which ones you respond to, which ones your body or your experience are going to say, "Yeah, that's the ticket. I like that one," and which ones you are going to say, "No, that doesn't make any sense to me or doesn't work for me." I'm going to start to develop some sense of what you respond to and I am going to start responding to your responses. Probably one of the most surprising things for me when I went to study with Erickson was how much he stressed observation.

Some of you may know of Ernie Rossi. He is a Jungian analyst who has written a lot with Erickson and about Erickson and has written his own ideas as well. He told me a great story one time

ELEMENTS OF SOLUTION-ORIENTED INDUCTION

- **Permission/Validation/Observation/Utilization**

  Any response/behavior/experience is valid.
  Any response can be evidence of hypnotic response or be the thing
  that leads to the hypnotic response.
  Permissive ("can," "might") vs. predictive ("will") or attributional
  ("are")
  Observing and incorporating responses

- **Evocation vs. Suggestion: The Naturalistic Approach**

- **Presupposition/Implication/Contextual Cues**

  Verbal presupposition: illusion of alternatives; before, during, and
  after; rate; awareness
  Behavioral presupposition
  Contextual cues
  Altering communication/behavior patterns

- **Matching**

  Nonverbal: rhythms, postures, voice qualities, breathing rate, ongoing observable behavior [mirroring/cross-mirroring]
  Verbal: vocabulary, syntax

- **Description**

  Videotalk
  Truisms

- **Permissive and Empowering Words**

  Possibility words
  Outline words
  Ronald Reagan words: unspecified as to person, place, time, thing,
  or action
  Directing attention and guiding associations

- **Splitting**

  Conscious/unconscious
  Here, present, external/there, past or future, internal
  Verbal and nonverbal

- **Linking**

  Verbal and nonverbal
  Bridging
  Re-evoking trance-like experiences

- **Interspersal**

  Nonverbal emphasis on words or phrases

that I really identify with because he said that when he went to study with Erickson, Erickson would either literally or metaphorically sort of jab him in the ribs with his elbow trying to get Ernie to pay attention. As soon as Erickson would start to talk, Ernie's gaze would start to drift up towards the ceiling. He was thinking about how Erickson was tapping into archetypes or how Erickson was doing something like recombining psychological DNA. Erickson would look over and there were Ernie's eyes on the ceiling and he would say, "Ernie, the subject is over there, there is no patient on the ceiling." You can hear Erickson, on one of the tapes, say, " . . . and you, Dr. Rossi, watch her face."

When Ernie told me that story, I thought that was exactly like me. My head was so full of theories that Erickson's training with me mostly consisted of getting me to watch people, listen to people, and not to spend so much time in my head with theories. Out there's where the data are.

So what we are trying to build up is this sense of responsiveness and you'll only know what they are responding to if you observe it. You won't notice if you are up there on the ceiling thinking about your theories.

So that's the first element, you give permission, validation, utilization. And in order to do that you've got to observe.

Evocation vs. Suggestion: The Naturalistic Approach

The second element is more of a philosophical difference than a technique. Instead of trying to program clients with the therapist's ideas from the outside, what we are really trying to do in Ericksonian hypnosis is what's called evocation. We are trying to evoke some experience from inside. In fact, that leads me to give you a definition of what hypnosis is. Hypnosis is the evocation of involuntary experience. That's one definition. I'll give you several definitions as the day goes on.

The Naturalistic Approach

Erickson sometimes called his hypnosis naturalistic hypnosis or naturalistic approaches to psychotherapy and I think what that meant was a couple of things. There are two sides to the naturalistic coin. One of those sides is that he thought people had natural abilities. He had a great trust in nature. He grew up on a farm and really loved nature and he thought people had many natural abilities and that you should respect and use those natural abilities. He thought people had natural abilities to go into trance and also natural abilities to experience trance phenomena.

Trance phenomena are things like amnesia, anesthesia, and time distortion, which we'll discuss in more detail later. Erickson believed that people learn these trance skills through common, everyday experiences. For example if you go to a suspense movie, you might forget about your headache. That's perhaps an experience of disassociation or anesthesia or analgesia. He thought that people had natural abilities to distort time, to change time. If you are waiting for a letter or a phone call you really want to have and it's taking what seems to be subjectively a long time, you've changed your experience of time. You do that naturally. In hypnosis, you can expand that capability and direct it. So the first part of this naturalistic approach is that people have natural abilities to go into trance and experience trance phenomena. They go in and out of common everyday trances. They've gone in and out of common everyday trances in their lives many times before you do a formal trance. You can trust their natural abilities.

The other side of the naturalistic coin is that trance induction doesn't have to be such a formalized "You will watch the watch" or ritualized thing. It can be a natural conversational approach and you will hear that again and again in the demonstrations I do and some of the work that I play of other people.

So in solution-oriented hypnosis we are not trying to teach people things from the outside; we are trying to evoke some experience from their insides. We are not trying to impose our ideas and beliefs, saying, in effect, "This is the way to resolve your problem" or "Here, take these new beliefs as they are much healthier than the ones you've got." We are trying to evoke natural experiences from inside people and expand and direct those experiences. I am not saying that we won't be influencing people and directing them, just that we are going to be influencing them in the direction of evoking their own experiences and using them towards achieving their own goals.

Presupposition / Implication / Contextual Cues

The next element and one that is probably in every trance induction and probably all of the psychotherapy I do is using presupposition, implication, and contextual cues. Implication was a big part of Erickson's work. Erickson was sometimes said to be a directive therapist. His work was very directive and at the same time, it was seen as indirect. How can it be directive and indirect at the same time?

Keep Them on the Road and Keep Them Moving

Erickson told a story about when he was growing up. Erickson had polio when he was 17, but before that he was a fairly active kid who lived in a farming area in Wisconsin for much of his growing up years. He told a story about how he was with friends one time a few miles away from his home. People didn't travel very far from their homes at that point and he and his friends were unfamiliar with this area. They were travelling down a country road and a horse which had obviously thrown it's rider ran past them. Its reins were all askew and it was very skittish. He and his friends chased the horse into a farmyard, and when they got into the farmyard, they caught the horse and calmed it down. Then Erickson announced, "I'm going to take this horse back home, back to its owner." His friends said, "We don't even know whose horse this is. How're you gonna do that?" Erickson said, "That's all right." He jumped up on the horse, told the horse to gid-dyup and the horse went out of the farmyard and took a right turn onto the road. Erickson spurred him on down the road. As they were riding down the road, every once in a while the horse tried to go off the road and eat some weed or some hay. Erickson just steered him back on the road and spurred him on. A few miles down the road, the horse turned and went into another farmyard. The farmer heard the commotion and came out and exclaimed, "That there's my horse. How did you know how to bring my horse home? I've never met you. You didn't know that was my horse." Erickson said,

"That's right, I didn't know where to bring the horse, but the horse knew the way. All I did was to keep him on the road and keep him moving." When he told that story, Erickson ended with the moral, "I think that's how you do psychotherapy."

I think that's a good model for how you can be directive and indirect at the same time. Erickson was very down on therapists imposing their values and beliefs and theories on people. He was very up on people getting moving in psychotherapy—that's what he thought was his job. You get them on the road and start them moving and they'll teach you by their responses. You keep them moving on the road to trance and their goals and then they'll let you know when they get there by their responses.

Probably the simplest way to understand implication and presupposition is to imagine that there's something that is going to happen or is happening or did happen. That's a good way to think of it. Like Shakti Gawain's creative visualizations. Visualize a goal and then you speak as if that goal is absolutely going to happen and then you can speculate within that certainty how that goal is going to be attained. Let's say that the certainty is that this person is going to go into trance. You visualize this person is going to go into trance. Then you can speak to the person about all the variations and possibilities about how he or she might go into trance: "I wonder if you'll go into trance quickly or if you'll go into trance slowly. I wonder if you'll go into trance with your eyes open or your eyes closed. Will you be able to hear everything I say as you go into trance, or will you drift off into your own experience going into trance? I don't really know," and so on.

Offer them a lot of speculation on the process of going into trance but never doubt, always presume and imply that they will go into trance.

Another way you can think about it, a way that my colleague Jim Wilk came up with, is to image that you are sitting in front of somebody and you are going to have to put them into trance. You are a little nervous because you are thinking, "Well maybe it won't work or maybe I won't be able to do it." So what you've got to do is give it up to a higher power. Give it up to Milton Erickson.

Imagine he is standing behind you and he is going to induce the trance because you know you're not up to it yet.

So Erickson is going to induce the trance and all I have to do is sit here in front of Glenn (*Bill sits in front of a participant in the front row*), and I can say to myself, "I can relax, Erickson's got it covered, he's behind me and he's going to do the trance, so all I have to do is speak to Glenn abut the possibilities of what's going to happen: 'Is that hand going to lift up to your face as you go into trance? I really don't know.'"

I'm going to be speculating to him like he's the folks at home and I'm the radio announcer calmly speculating about how the game's going to go but I already know that he's going to go into trance because Erickson's got that taken care of. Or I might be working on the assumption that Erickson has already told me that he is going to do a trance induction and he's going to do, during this trance induction, a hand levitation. I know Glenn's going to get a hand levitation and I'm going to be speculating out loud: "Will it be the right hand or will it be the left hand? Will one of those hands start to lift up or will both of those hands start to lift up? I really don't know. Will you feel a thumb move first, a finger move first?"

I'm just going to speculate on the possibilities of how it will happen. I'm never going to doubt that the hand levitation is going to happen. I'm never going to doubt that the trance induction is going to happen. I am just going to speculate on the possible variations that can take place while it is happening. That's one way of thinking about it, so all of your speaking will be from the certainty that it's going to happen. The certainty that this goal over here is going to happen and you can doubt anything on the way like whether it would be the right hand or the left hand, whether it would be slow or whether you'll notice that it's happening or whether you won't notice that it's happening, whether you believe that it happens, whether you won't believe that it happens, what kind of rate at which it will happen. So all of those are verbal presuppositions.

Let me give you another handout (1.2), one that will summarize some common presuppositions that are used in hypnosis. This one is "Using Presupposition in Hypnosis."

Handout 1.2

USING PRESUPPOSITION IN HYPNOSIS

1. Give two or more options that lead in the desired direction.

   –Would you like to go into trance now or later?
   –I don't know if you'd like to close your eyes to go into a trance of if you'll keep your eyes open.
   –Would you like to use the recliner or stay where you're seated to go into a trance?

2. Presume that something is about to happen.

   –Before you go into trance, there are some myths about hypnosis that I'd like to dispel.
   –Have you ever been in trance before?
   –When you're in trance, you can do something nice for yourself.
   –Don't go into trance too quickly.

3. Presume that something is happening.

   –You can go deeper.
   –That's right, just continuing.
   –As your unconscious mind continues to help you do what you need to do . . .

4. Presume that something just happened.

   –How was that?
   –Welcome back!
   –How did that trance compare with the last one?
   –. . . and your unconscious mind can now solve other problems that we haven't even talked about.

5. Imply that something is happening, will happen, or just happened by talking about its rate of occurrence.

   –Don't go in too quickly.
   –I don't know when your unconscious will solve that for you.

6. Imply that something is happening, will happen, or just happened and wonder aloud whether that person is aware of that.

   –I don't know whether you have noticed that your breathing has changed.
   –You probably aren't aware that your unconscious mind is doing a lot of work for you.

Verbal presupposition has a couple of categories. One of them is called the Illusion of Alternatives. This was initially called the Illusion of Choice by Lawrence Kubie, who wrote some articles with Erickson many years ago. The Illusion of Alternatives technique involves giving two or more choices in which either of the choices that is offered leads to the desired result. Parents all over the world know this technique. It's "Would you like to watch 15 more minutes of television or have a bedtime story before you go to sleep?" Two or more alternatives are offered and any of the alternatives that are chosen lead in the desired direction: "Would you like to go into a light trance, medium trance, or a deep trance? Would you like to go into a trance with your legs crossed, or would you like to uncross your legs? Would you like to take your glasses off to go into trance, or would you rather keep them on?" All of that is going to presuppose that they are going to go into trance and we are just negotiating what the preferred way is for them to go into trance: "Is your conscious mind going to know that you are going into trance or not know that you are going into trance?"

AUDIENCE: Is it always two?

No, it could be three, four, or five. "Would you like to go into light trance, medium trance, or deep trance" uses three. Sometimes it will be a whole string. You'll hear that in the demonstrations and taped examples later.

Another type of presupposition, one I like quite a bit, is the "Before, During, and After" set of presuppositions. Before, during, and after presuppositions imply or suggest without stating it obviously or directly that you are just about to go into this stuff called trance, or that you are in this experience called trance, or that you've just been in this experience called trance.

Now maybe here's a good place to demystify trance a little. If a Martian anthropologist came down and observed what we do during this process we call hypnosis, the Martian anthropologist would only see a conversation, would only hear a conversation. I'm usually speaking in my normal hyperactive—I mean kinetic—sort of way and then, all of a sudden, at some point in the conversation I start to slow down, I start to talk to your conscious mind

. . . your unconscious mind . . . I talk about one part of you . . . and then the other part of you . . . and then there's another point where I start to talk in my normal kinetic sort of way again. So nonverbally and verbally I'm going to imply that this is a different conversation. Actually it's one long conversation and all the Martian can see and hear is that at one point I start to talk funny and you start to act funny during that conversation and then I start to talk and act like I did before and you start to act and talk like you did in the first part of the conversation.

There's a big debate in the hypnosis field that's not settled yet between the state theorists and the non-state theorists. Erickson was a state theorist. The state theorists say there is such a state as trance. And the non-state theorists say there's no need for that construct. T. X. Barber is one of the most well known non-state theorists. He holds that you don't need the construct of hypnosis or trance to explain what happens during one of these conversations.

A bunch of the non-state folks are social psychologists and think that trance is just a social psychological phenomenon, that it's not an internal state at all, it's a way of interacting. Jay Haley, some years ago, wrote about the interactional explanation of hypnosis and certainly there is a case to be made for that. I guess you could say that there is bad news and good news about all this. The bad news for all of you is that you are in a hypnosis workshop, you've paid your money, you've gotten here, and there is no such thing as hypnosis. So far the state theorists haven't proved that there is such a thing as hypnosis. They haven't found those consistent brain waves for hypnosis yet, like they have in meditation. There are no other consistent physiological measures that are generally accepted that prove that there is such a thing as trance. So the non-state theorists are winning the debate so far. The state theorists have to prove that there is such a state as hypnosis and they haven't yet.

Actually I agree with both points of view because for me being a social constructivist, I think that trance isn't a **thing** at all. It's a distinguished state in language. It's just like they haven't been able to measure love yet but you know when you're in it and other people can usually tell when you're in it, but they haven't measured it physiologically yet. There could be non-state theorists and state theorists of love, too, and what I would say about it is it's distinguished linguistically and you start to name it. If you didn't know the name "love" for the experience you were having, maybe you would think you had the flu or something because you felt weird. But after you give it the name "love" and it's sort of associated with certain situations again and again, you have the sense that it's this stuff called love and it works. It's the same thing with trance. So the bad news is there is no such thing as trance and the good news is it doesn't seem to matter much for clinical work because I know when you are in one, I can teach you to recognize when people are in one, I know when I'm in one and that seems to work for clinical purposes.

What you are trying to do in using the before, during, and after presuppositions is to build up the idea that there is a thing called trance; that it is a distinct state linguistically and experientially. Partly how you do that is you imply that it's about to happen, that it is happening, and that it just happened and you do that linguistically. You can do it behaviorally and interactionally also, but we'll get to that in a minute. Let's stick with the linguistic ways first.

Let me give you an example.

THERAPIST: Bob, I am going to ask you a couple of questions. Have you been in trance? One of these formal kind of trances?

BOB: I think so.

Okay. Now let me ask you a different question that sounds somewhat the same: "Have you ever been in trance before?" Now it could be the same answer, but the implication was different. Because, "Have you ever been in trance *before*" implies that sometime in the future you are going to go into trance—especially given the context if we are in a hypnosis session, if we are in a psychotherapy session, if we have already discussed that we are going to do hypnosis. The implication is that you are going to go into trance. But I haven't said, "You are going into trance." It is just implied.

I might say, "Before you go into trance, there are a few myths of hypnosis that I want to talk to you about." That sounds like a fairly reasonable thing to say. It doesn't sound like a hypnotic suggestion, but it is a suggestion, a suggestion that you are going to go into trance because I said "**before** you go into trance." Those are some of the "before" presuppositions.

Then you have the "During" presuppositions. The "during" ones are what I'm going to use when I start to see some signs that the person is showing trance responses or hypnotic responses. (I'll give you a list of those later.) Once I start to see those signs, I'm going to start to imply that you are already in this state called trance and start to talk as if you are in it. So I might say, "That's right, you can go deeper." Now if I were in the middle of a conversation with you, why would I say, "That's right, go deeper?" What are you supposed to go deeper into, the conversation? I'm going to imply that we are having this conversation called trance and in the middle of this there is something different happening: "You can go deeper. You can go all the way in." Why would I say that in the middle of a conversation? It would be a weird thing to say. But if I had already distinguished this stuff called hypnosis or trance, it's not such a weird thing to say. Also we use a lot of spatial metaphors for hypnosis and for the mind in general. We say, "Go **deeper**, go all the way **in**." Same thing for the mind. Where's the **back** of your mind, as in when you have something in the "back of your mind?" Where's **deep** thinking; where do you do you "deep thinking?" So we use spatial metaphors. There is no such space as trance but we use spatial metaphors to understand it, to make sense of it.

At a certain point I'm going to imply that trance is over, that this part of the conversation is over. So I might say, "Welcome back." Now why would I, again, say "Welcome back" during the middle of a conversation unless something has just ended? I might say, "How was that?" If you were having sex with somebody and they said, "How was that?" it would imply that the sex was over, right? Maybe you thought you were in the middle of that conversation. (*Laughter*) I see some of you have had this experience. If we say, "How was that," it implies that something just ended in the conversation. Something is over—something gets distinguished by these words and this thing is called hypnosis or trance or a relaxed state. Whatever name you give it, that's how it gets distinguished. By the end of this workshop, those of you who haven't been making the distinction called trance will start to make it a lot more.

Because we are talking about it so much and I'll be showing it so much, it will start to be distinguished in your experience.

One of the things I realized once I made the distinction called trance is how often my clients were putting me in trance, and how to bring myself out of trance once I made that distinction. I also noticed how often my clients were spontaneously going into what I called trance, and how often in common, everyday life I was going into trance and other people were going into trance. So, I started to make this distinction. I don't know what I was noticing before when my clients were doing this; obviously not that because I never made that distinction. But now I notice it a lot. Once you make the distinction, you will start to notice it quite a bit.

AUDIENCE: You mean while I'm daydreaming I'm in a type of trance?

It depends on the daydream. I would start to observe you and perhaps what you call a daydream I might call a mini-trance if it has some characteristics of what I call trance. After a while you will start to make that distinction. Not everything is a trance. Some things aren't. That was an idea I heard when I went to some of my first workshops on this stuff, that everybody is always in a trance. You could construe it that way but that dilutes the definition of trance for me. I went to one of the early workshops on Ericksonian stuff, and I watched the tape called "The Artistry of Milton Erickson." I was watching the first segment of it, and I was fading as I watched it and I thought, "Boy, I was really in a trance watching that because I missed three quarters of it." Later I realized, "No, I was just asleep." I was bored, you know? I thought I must be in a trance because they were talking about trance so much, but after I started to make the distinction as the years went on, I realized the difference between sleep and trance. It wasn't a distinction I made earlier on. If you are daydreaming you'll think, "I must be in a trance." But after you go into some trances and start to make the distinction again and again, you'll be able to tell whether you were in trance or not. That will be something you decide experientially and observationally.

Not only can you do implication linguistically but you can do it nonverbally because, again, there will be a certain point **WHEN I'LL BE TALKING LIKE THIS** and then a certain point when I'll be talking like this. So, behaviorally, I'm going to imply that there is a different conversation going on here, and then I'm going to imply when my behavior changes again that this is no longer a trance conversation. After a while in this workshop all I'll have to do is look at some of you meaningfully and say, "That's right," and you'll start to feel yourself go into a trance, because it'll be enough of a contextual cue that this is trance talk. Probably right now, unless some of you have been to other Ericksonian workshops, that's not much of a contextual cue for you, but it starts to get built up by association as a contextual cue.

When I work in my office, I have these sort of deadly florescent lights on and, then, when I turn on the incandescent light on the desk and turn off the big lights, that's a contextual cue for "It's time to do a trance." When trance is over I turn on the big lights again and turn off the other light. The next time the person comes into the office and I turn on the incandescent light and turn off the fluorescent lights, it tends to be a cue. Usually they move over to the reclining chair, although it's not always available because I sometimes use different offices, and it's not necessary. Usually people move over to the recliner and go into trance. So as soon as I just gesture to the reclining chair, that's all the trance induction that has to be done after a while. They go to the chair, they close their eyes, they start to go into their own trance. I turn off the overhead lights and turn on the incandescent light. That is what I mean by a contextual cue: This cue is in the context before trance (when the fluorescent lights are on), this cue is present during trance (the incandescent lights are on), and the cue after trance is when the fluorescent lights are on again. So, in addition to linguistic cues, we start to make behavioral and contextual cues that indicate that this is **trance** and this is **not trance.**

There are a couple of other linguistic suggestions, implications, presuppositions that we can talk about; one of them is the awareness one. When you use phrases like, "I don't know whether you are aware . . . " or "I don't know if you realize . . . " or "I don't know whether you've noticed . . . ," anything you say after those phrases is implied. That's what's presupposed. "I don't know whether you've noticed how quickly you are going into trance. I don't know whether you've noticed your responses so far. I don't know whether you realize that your unconscious mind is doing a lot of thinking for you. I don't know whether you've noticed that your breathing has changed." All you are doing is asking or wondering or speculating about whether they've noticed it, you're not questioning whether or not it is actually happening. You are only questioning whether they have noticed or not. That's another type of presupposition.

Another presupposition, one that's related to the before, during, and after ones is **rate**. "I don't want you to go into trance too soon tonight," Erickson says on one of his tapes, "Not yet. . . . " "Don't sit down on the chair yet." We are not doubting that the person will go into trance or sit down on the chair, we are just talking about the rate—how quickly, how soon. Those are rate presuppositions.

There are other types of presuppositions, but it would take too long to detail all of them, so let's move on to the next element of induction, which is matching.

Matching

Matching is just joining your body behavior and language behavior to other people's body behavior and language behavior. Bandler and Grinder make a nice distinction about this. They divide it into *mirroring* and *cross mirroring*. **Mirroring** is when you do things like take the same body posture or you breathe at the same rate as the other person does. Essentially, it's like miming. You take exactly the same posture they do, you nod when they nod, you pick up the pen in your hand and start to take notes when they do. That's like a mime. When they breathe, you breathe. When they nod, you nod. Anything that changes in their behavior you match exactly.

There is another kind of matching called **cross mirroring**, and that's when you don't exactly take the same posture as they do or breathe at the same rate as they do, but something in your behavior varies along something in their behavior so you co-vary. I used to work in crisis counseling and some people would come in or call me on the phone and they would be breathlessly yelling, "aa!!!@#%$%$#@#$$$," and I don't want to breathe the same way they breathe or I may have a crisis myself or maybe pass out. They are breathing at a rate that doesn't support feeling calm. They are breathing in a way that freaks them out. So instead of breathing the same way they breathe, I may nod each time they exhale or nod in time to their breathing. I don't have to take the same body posture. Instead, maybe every time their body moves to one side I could lift up my hand a little. Something about my behavior varies along with something about their behavior. That's cross mirroring.

Not only are we talking physical or biological matching, but it can be linguistic as well. This can be accomplished by using the same words they use, using the same syntax that they use. "I don't know nothing about nothing," a client says. "So that tells me you don't know nothing about not going into a trance," I reply. One part of the linguistic matching involves the hypnotist mirroring the language and syntax that the person is using.

Description

You can also use what I call "Descriptive Matching." Descriptive matching can be best illustrated by using an analogy. Imagine that you are a radio commentator who is describing the action in this sport of hypnosis to the folks at home with their ears to the radio. You are going to describe the game using only terms that indicate the actions going on on the field. Don't go beyond what you can see and hear. Strange but true, though, in this game, the folks at home happen to be the person that's sitting in front of you. So I'm going to describe for Glenn, as if he is the folks at home, what's happening in the game so far—but only those things that I can observe as if I could see them and hear them on a videotape. I'm not going beyond that. I won't say to Glenn, "You're sitting in a very relaxed way. Listening very attentively." That's getting into his insides, claiming that I have X-ray vision and can see that he is relaxed and attentive. I'm just going to stay with his outside: "You're sitting in a chair, blinking, head moving, nodding, your facial muscles moving. Your hand holding a pen, hand holding a recorder, some part of your body touching another part of your body, nodding . . . breathing." That's all the stuff I can see. But if I say, "Breathing in a very comfortable way," I've gone beyond what I can see and hear. Descriptive matching is telling people the truth about what you see and hear from your perspective. It's sort of operating as a human biofeedback machine. I'm just going to tell you what it is that I see and hear. That can have several effects. One is I'm going to get some credibility with you because I'm telling you the truth and not going beyond the truth, and I'm not jarring or intruding upon your experience. The second thing is that my describing your body and the immediate environment is going to start to narrow your focus of attention. Another definition of trance is a narrowing of focus of attention. That's not the only way but that's one way. Descriptive matching is the last aspect of matching, and if you go beyond descriptive matching I suggest you go into the next category, which I call "Permissive and Empowering Words."

Permissive and Empowering Words

If you are going to go beyond what you can actually describe to people and what's credible for them in terms of just being able to see and hear, you want to be able to talk to people in a way that you don't intrude unhelpfully on their experience or jar them out of trance by saying something that doesn't fit for them. For example, the person sitting in front of you may appear very relaxed, but inside they may be feeling very anxious, or very aware of their heart beating. If you assume you can read their mind, you may be wrong. To counteract this difficulty, you can use "packaged words."

I call them packaged words because it's as if you have a package that's got a label written on it. It arrives in your office from UPS and the label reads "experience." Now what does the word experience mean? It's very vague. That is, it's not specified as to person, place, time, thing, or action. It's not very specific in terms of specific things you can point to in the world. It's not sensory-based. So you get this package and you don't know what's in it unless you open the package and unpack it in terms of the specific person, place, thing, time, or action. You don't know what's in that pack-

age. Sometimes I call these words "Ronald Reagan words" because
they sound so specific but they don't really mean anything. You
probably learned in your counseling training to be concrete and
specific. You know, Carkhuff and Truax-land. It's a great idea and
certainly has it's place. This technique, though, is the exact opposite of that. There is a time to be concrete and specific and very
sensory-based and there is a time to be vague as hell and this is the
time to be vague as hell. The time to be vague is when you want to
open up the possibility for people to create their own experience
and when you don't want to intrude upon people's experience by
the words that you use.

Even though these words are vague, they are not totally wishy-
washy. It's going to be more like Garrison Keillor on Prairie Home
Companion or any of the old radio theatre programs. You are
going to give just enough detail for people to create their own
experience and guide them in certain directions. You are not going
to say, "You can think about anything, anytime, and anyplace"—
that's a little too vague. You're going to talk about somewhat spe-
cific-sounding things and then channel their experience and guide
their associations in certain directions. You'll be directing their
inner activities a little without imposing or intruding so much.
That's what Garrison Keillor does. If you saw a movie of Lake
Wobegon you'd probably be a little disappointed because he's just
giving you enough to create your own images and ideas of Lake
Wobegon. And that's the idea here—to give people enough guid-
ance and an outline so they can fill in the inside and color inside of
the lines on their own.

Another way to do it is to include the opposite, the "or not." If
you sense that the person is sitting there relaxed you could say,
"And you could be sitting there in a very comfortable way and you
don't have to be comfortable." Or if you say something that sounds
specific and you get a response from the person that indicates what
you said is not right for them, you can correct it by including the
opposite possibility. So if you happen to say, "And you are sitting
there very comfortably," and you notice their brow furrowing, you
can say, " . . . or maybe you're not comfortable, I really don't
know." You can give them permission to feel comfortable or not
comfortable or both. You could give them permission to feel com-

fortable **and** not comfortable. We'll be talking about that when we talk about trance logic.

Erickson's Tag Questions

Erickson would sometimes use tag questions. Tag questions are little phrases at the end of a sentence that turn statements into questions. You'll hear this in one of the examples that we'll play, when Erickson says to a subject, " . . . and you're very comfortable, are you not?" He thought it was really important to include the "No" along with the "Yes." He thought the therapist should say the "No" before the client or subject had a chance to. I saw the Milan Family Therapists do some presentations on their way of working with families and when giving an interpretation, they say, "So Johnny, he takes care of the whole family, no?" They take back everything that they say as soon as they say it. "He keeps the family stable, no?" The British have a similar phrase: "Isn't it?"; the French have "N'est-ce pas?"

Now I'm going to play the first in a series of audiotaped examples of Ericksonian hypnosis. The point of my playing these tapes and the videotapes you will see later is to give you a number of different people and styles to model, not just my own, which you'll see in demonstrations. I don't want you to come away from this workshop a Bill O'Hanlon clone or a Milton Erickson clone. This is a general orientation and I'd like you to find your own style within it.

This first example is Erickson and it's from the tape that accompanies the book *Hypnotic Realities*. Ernie Rossi recorded Erickson working with Sheila Rossi, who was then Ernie's wife. She is also a psychologist and her name is also Dr. Rossi, so when you hear Erickson elbowing Ernie Rossi in the ribs saying, "Now you, Dr. Rossi, watch her face," it's both a message to Ernie to observe and, it seems, a dissociation suggestion for Sheila. In this example, you'll be able to hear some of the elements that we've been talking about, focusing attention, guiding associations, and implying certain things with his voice and using these vague and empty words.

Sheila has come in to learn hypnosis, but unlike her husband Ernie, who likes to learn intellectually, she wants to learn experientially. She wants to learn from the inside out, so what does he do? He brings her back to something in her childhood, this is the *evocation* approach, tells her that she's been able to learn this very complicated thing, learning how to read and write and learning how to recognize all those letters, and she's learned it, she's learned a complicated thing, she learned it so it became automatic for her so she had perfect mental images so she could recall all those images whenever she needed them. This is going to be an evocation of an earlier experience that she can use to learn this new stuff that's very complicated, but that she can learn automatically, unconsciously.

Audiotape Example #1:
Milton Erickson — Basic Induction

. . . Look at the far upper corner of that picture. Now you, Dr. Rossi, watch her face. The far upper corner of that picture. Now I'm going to talk to you. When you first went to kindergarten, grade school, this matter of learning letters and numerals seemed to be a big insurmountable task. To recognize the letter A, to tell a Q from an O was very, very difficult. And then too, script and print were so different. But you learned to form a mental image of some kind. You didn't know it at the time, but it was a permanent mental image. And later on in grammar school you formed other mental images of words or pictures of sentences. You developed more and more mental images without knowing you were developing mental images. And you can recall all those images. Now you can go anywhere you wish, and transport yourself to any situation. You can feel water. You may want to swim in it. . . .

Now that's very permissive, she doesn't have to go anywhere, she doesn't have to transport herself, she doesn't have to feel water, she doesn't have to swim in it, these are all possibilities and she might pick any of them or she might pick none of them.

You can do anything you want. . . .

That's a nice expression, and especially the way he says it—it sounds like a little kid, doesn't it?—declaring, "I can do anything I want." It somewhat implies again that she's going to regress back to childhood. This time it's evoked by certain words, phrases, and tonal expressions.

You don't even have to listen to my voice because your un-conscious will hear it. Your unconscious can try anything it wishes. But your conscious mind isn't going to do anything of importance. You will notice that your conscious mind is somewhat concerned since it keeps fluttering your eyelids. But you have altered your rate of breathing. You've altered your pulse. You've altered your blood pressure. And without knowing . . . it you're demonstrating the immobility that a hypnotic subject can show. . . .

That last little segment introduces the next piece that I want to teach and that is the use of what I call **splitting**. In this particular aspect of splitting we are going to be focusing on using splitting for induction, but later on we are going to use it in other areas of hypnosis and hypnotherapy.

Splitting

Splitting is distinguishing between two things that haven't been distinguished before or separating into parts something that was seen as a unified thing. Typically, the split that's proposed in induc-tion in this particular approach is a split between the **conscious mind** and the **unconscious mind**. Now I want you to keep in mind that these are linguistic splits and distinctions, not distinctions in the real world. They have done a lot of autopsies and never found any unconscious minds inside anybody or conscious minds inside anybody. It's just like left brain, right brain. They've never found any right brains or left brains either. They just found little creases there. The distinction "right brain or left brain" is made up by human beings and language, biology didn't make that one up. Hu-man beings make these distinctions up. It's like T.A. I was joking yesterday that when T.A. was popular, people would come into my office and talk in T.A. terms. It was if they had three little circles tattooed on them, P, A, and C. But they've never found those in autopsies and they are not real. There are no parents inside you. It's made up linguistically. It may be a useful way to distinguish your experience, but it's made up. Descartes proposed the mind/body split and a lot of people bought it, but there's no such split in the world as "mind/body."

So conscious and unconscious is first going to be proposed as a split, then we are going to lead in the direction of the unconscious mind, and then we want people to come out of trance and we are going to lead in the direction of the conscious mind. First we just propose a split and we do that verbally and nonverbally, so listen and watch as I do this:

CONSCIOUSLY YOU MAY NOT REALLY KNOW WHAT IT MEANS TO GO INTO A TRANCE, your unconscious mind may have a lot of experience already **going into a trance. SO CONSCIOUSLY YOU COULD BE SITTING THERE WONDERING WHETHER THIS IS GOING INTO A TRANCE** and your unconscious mind could already be helping you **go into a trance.**

What I've done is to talk about you as if you have two parts, conscious and unconscious but, at the same time, I've done it nonverbally and verbally. I've done it nonverbally by doing the conscious mind over here (*leaning to the right side*) and the unconscious mind over here (*leaning to the left side*). Conscious mind with *this* voice tone, voice value, this facial expression, and *this* special location and voice tone for the unconscious mind. Now you don't have to do it that particular way. It just happens that I and most of the people who studied with Erickson do it that way because we sat in front of Erickson who, near the end of his life when he was really disabled with the aftereffects of polio and some of the muscle deterioration that happened, did it that way.

He had learned earlier on in his career to use his voice in a very precise way. So, later on, when he would have a muscle spasm and his body would move here and there uncontrollably, he'd learned to use that to mark things out and emphasize things in this way.

He'd have a spasm and talk about the unconscious mind over here. He'd have another muscle spasm and talk about the conscious mind over there. Those of us who sat in front of him in trance for years or months or days or whatever it was, developed this sort of Erickson bob and weave that we do, as we modelled on that particular technique. Sort of like Ray Charles doing trance or something, we talk about the conscious mind over here and the unconscious mind over here and the conscious mind over here—we distinguish it verbally and nonverbally. To induce the trance, then, we lead over here into unconscious land for a while and talk about the unconscious, using those "unconscious" voice tones and voice volumes and facial expressions that I use. And then when it's time to come out of trance, we lead back to the conscious mind.

In a similar way, we initially begin with an external focus of attention and a here-and-now focus, and then go in a direction of an internal focus of attention. And instead of here and now, go to there-and-then—any place other than here, at any time other than now, the past or the future. So you might direct a person's attention toward an internal focus by saying, "Perhaps you haven't yet noticed a particular feeling of warmth in one of your hands or both of them." Closing your eyes automatically directs your attention internally, for most people. "There and then" can be yesterday, or when you were four years old, or two weeks from now—anytime other than here and now. I may tell a story about learning to write, how hard it was initially to hold that pencil and make those lines the correct way. How, at first, "b" and "d" looked the same and were easily confused, while now I don't even think about which is which, it's automatic. The common experience of learning to identify letters of the alphabet has occurred in childhood for all of us (unless perhaps you've just recently learned to read). And so the story directs the person's attention to a time in the past, split from the present here and now.

We can also make a split between *now*, when the particular problem is present, to a time in the future when the problem is no longer present.

We start to lead in that direction—internal, there and then, and, likewise, when it's time to come out of trance, we lead in the opposite direction and bring people back to a more external focus of attention, the more here-and-now focus. First, we propose a split, then we move on to one side of the split, and then we move back to the other side of the split to come out of trance.

Splitting is making distinctions and disassociating certain things that have been associated or making a distinction in a unified element and breaking it up into pieces. You are the unified element and we are going to propose that you split yourself up into pieces — the conscious and unconscious aspects of your experience.

Linking

A complementary skill is **linking**. Linking is joining two things together that haven't been joined before. You can do linking verbally and nonverbally, as well. There are various kinds of linkages that one could propose.

First, there are usually several levels of verbal linking: (1) **conjunction** — where you put two things together by using a conjunction in between them: "You are sitting in the chair and you can go into trance." Now there is nothing about sitting in a chair that makes you go into trance inherently, but as soon as I propose that linkage it's a little more likely: "You're sitting in a chair, listening to my voice, and you can go into a trance." Now if I want to make a stronger implied connection, I can use what we call a (2) **contingent suggestion** or **contingent linkage**. Contingent linking has two typical forms. One is "as," "while," and "when": "As you're sitting in that chair, listening to my voice, you can go into trance," "When you sit all the way down in that chair, you can go all the way into trance," "As you sit all the way down in that chair you can go all the way into trance," "While your conscious mind is listening and wondering whether you are going into trance, your unconscious mind can help you go into trance." So it's implying some sort of linkage between those two or three things that are happening.

The other kind of **contingent linking** is "the more this, the more that" or "the less this, the less that" or "the more this, the less that." So I could say, "The more your conscious mind is distracted by the sounds in the room, the easier it can be for your unconscious mind to help you go into trance, since it's freed up from the domination of your conscious mind." There the link is the more you are distracted, the more you go into trance. That's a good linkage to propose if they are going to be distracted. That's contingent linking.

The strongest level of linkage is (3) **causal linkage** in which you claim that something causes or will cause another thing. I rarely use this strong linkage, for the reasons I mentioned earlier, because the person might feel coerced or you or they might fail. Sometimes you can use cause and effect, and the way I usually use it is about things that can't be checked, like "Being in trance will make your unconscious mind do a lot of creative thinking." It is not very easy to check that kind of thing. Sometimes I call solution-oriented hypnosis "hypnosis for chickens." It is not animal hypnosis, you know, for chickens, but it is for chicken therapists who don't want to fail or have their clients fail. So we are trying to create a context where it is impossible for you to fail. You just can't fail at doing this because we create this climate and this opportunity for you to do this, and we incorporate whatever it is that you are responding to.

There are other kinds of linking that can be used. I talked about **incorporating** earlier — incorporating clients' objections or their behavior. That's a utilization approach. **Bridging** is that technique Erickson used with the guy who was pacing back and forth, he bridged from where the guy was, this nervous guy who couldn't sit down and get therapy, into a guy who was sitting down and going into trance. By putting little stepping stones across what seemed an uncrossable river, one stepping stone was hesitating a little in front of the chair, the other one was linking comfort to the chair, another one was speaking slower so the guy could walk slower, Erickson linked each of those elements in there to help the guy get to where he was going. Utilize where the person is *now*, based on their own report and/or their observed behavior, and bridge it to trance. Notice where the person is at, validate that, and bridge it over to trance, by using small steps rather than trying to make that one big leap.

The last category under the heading of linking is **re-evoking trance-like experiences**. Evoking, helping the person evoke, typical everyday trance-like experiences like driving a car long distance where you go into that highway hypnosis kind of thing, or sitting in a movie theater so lost in the movie that you don't realize time is going by. Those are common everyday trance experiences that you can evoke and link to the trance. You may have the person recall some typical trance-like experience, or you may tell a story about a trance-like experience of your own, or of another person that is a common experience, and evoke it that way. Of course, if a person has been in trance before, you can re-evoke that experience itself.

Interspersal

The last element on that sheet that you have is the interspersal technique. It is a combination of splitting and linking. Let me give you an example that Erickson gave when he was doing supervision with me that was really memorable. He said that some patient in the mental hospital gave the staff this note:

I am going to a place where there are no bad **mad** people.

He gave it to me and several people that were there, and he said, "What was the patient trying to say to us?" So he gave me the note and I looked at it upside down and I tried several creative interpretations, and he snatched it out of my hand and said, "You've failed miserably at that." Those of you who've read *Taproots*, don't give it away, because the answer's in there. (*Participant: I've got one idea: "I am going mad."*) That's exactly right, that's the answer. You are right, for $100,000. Bzzzzzt. **I am going mad**. Why is that distinguished? Because it has darker letters. Erickson made the riddle a little harder because all he did was make it a little darker and he had really bad handwriting.

The guy in the mental hospital was so afraid of articulating his thought that he was going to go mad, he figured if he said it out loud, he would go mad, so he had to disguise it in some way. He gave it to the staff and all the staff passed it around and couldn't get it. Erickson, of course, figured it out, brilliant genius that he was, because these words were slightly emphasized. Now, I've made it a lot more obvious making them bold for you. Embedded in this larger message is a sub-message, a subtext, that says, "I am going mad."

Erickson figured if patients can do this multiple-level communication, why can't therapists? Why can't hypnotists? His example
made it very memorable for me. So, he made up a hypnotic technique called **interspersal** where in the entire text he would make a
subtext that was emphasized nonverbally in some way that would
emphasize suggestions. If he wanted a person (this is a silly example) to scratch their nose, he might say, using voice emphasis:
"Now everybody **knows** that in hypnosis you have to start from
scratch." A serious example is the case in which you want to help a
person with back spasms or back pain relax the muscles in their
back. So you might say:

> "Now you might be able to remember **back** to a time when
> you were more **relaxed**. Or more **comfortable**, I really don't
> know. But somewhere in your **background** you have experi-
> ences of **relaxation**, you have experiences of **comfort**."

Now what have I emphasized here? Back—relaxed, back—comfort, back—comfortable. That's interspersal.

> "And I really don't know how tense your **muscles** might be
> right now, but I do know that some time in the past your
> **muscles** have been **relaxed** and those **relaxed** **muscles** in your
> **background** can really help you in the future to be more **com-
> fortable**, to be more **relaxed**. Even though you consciously
> can't imagine how your **back** could feel more **comfortable**."

I've emphasized certain words: **back, relaxed, muscles relaxed,
back relaxed, muscles comfortable**. When I emphasize those
words, they become interspersed, indirect suggestions. You can
emphasize by tone of voice, volume, or rate of speech, by location—the Erickson bob and weave we talked about earlier, for
example—by any nonverbal means. By touching their arm at certain words, or by moving your hand or some other body part if the
person has her eyes open. Some people call this interspersal technique "analogical marking"—it's the same thing.
If I wanted to use this technique in induction, one of the things I
might do, especially if you are worried or skeptical or didn't think

you could go into trance, is say to you, "now I really don't know if you consciously believe that you can **go into a trance**, I really don't know if you are certain how **deeply** you could **go into a trance**. And if you really know how **quickly** you could **go into a trance**." What have I said? I've just been talking about their skepticism, but the words I've been emphasizing are: *go into a trance, go deeply into a trance, go quickly into a trance, go into a trance*. On one level I'm just matching their conscious skepticism and on another level I'm giving them suggestions about going into a trance.

I hope I don't have to convince you that this technique is to be used for the client's benefit, not for your benefit. I was at a swap meet one time and I was walking around what was like a glorified garage sale, but they also had some commercial exhibits. One guy was selling knives that were sort of like Ginsu knives. He had these knives and he was doing this demonstration, and he had a little wireless mic on and he was doing a demo. He said, "Ladies and gentlemen, the handles on these knives, even though they are plastic, are very strong." At that he took a hammer and pounded it on the handle. The hammer bounced off. Pretty impressive. He had this crowd around him, entranced. I was standing at the back of the crowd watching his sales strategies. Then he said, "Ladies and gentlemen, if you take this knife and you put it down your garbage disposal and you turn on your garbage disposal, do you know what happens?" (You figure he's going to say that nothing happens, the knives are intact.) Instead he says, in a very dramatic voice, "Ladies and gentlemen, it **chews it**!" I was so shocked that I literally jumped back and watched to see if anybody else noticed what he had just said, but they were all just sort of listening to his spiel, and he just went on as if nothing had happened. I walked around the swap meet and when I came back around he was doing the same spiel, using the same exact words. When he got to that part, I listened to hear if he did it the same and he said, "It **chews it**!" I looked at him and caught his eyes for a moment, to see if he knew that he was dong this and he didn't seem to have any idea. But he knew enough to do it the same way each time because it sold a lot of knives. He was emphasizing the words **chews it** (**choose it**) in that particular presentation. Buy this knife, choose it. He didn't realize he was doing that.

Now, I don't want advertisers to use this, but if you are going to try to sell things to clients that are for their own benefit, that are to help them achieve their goals, then I don't have an ethical objection to the use of this technique. That's why I think it's important to use these techniques, all of them, in an ethical way. What I mean by "ethical" is influencing them not for your benefit, but for their benefit. Of course you are going to benefit if they get better, but I'm saying don't use them merely or mainly for your benefit, as in getting them to do things that they don't want to do or are inappropriate for them to do.

The interspersal technique is the last basic element in the list. Those are the basic building blocks that you are going to use to put together a trance induction today. Perhaps at this point it seems a bit overwhelming, but take my word for it, you will soon be using these elements as we get you to do some exercises incorporating them, one by one, into your repertoire.

What I have tried to do in this introduction is demystify hypnotic induction for you. Sometimes I'm not even sure that hypnosis is the right word to use for what we are doing during this process. Perhaps "solution-oriented inner work" would be a better term, but I was trained in the tradition of hypnosis, so I call it hypnosis.

Erickson sometimes did what is called "conversational" or "informal" induction. That is when the induction is interwoven into a natural conversation setting or a lecture. The listener is not ever alerted to the fact that an induction is occurring. If you listen to many of Erickson's lectures, you will hear many of the elements I have been teaching this morning included within the structure of his lecture. I rarely do this kind of induction as I have ethical objections to it, but many Ericksonians do use it.

Because conversational inductions do not include the ritualized elements that most formal inductions do (like sitting down in a chair, closing your eyes, rolling your eyes back in your head, breathing deeply, etc.), this technique shows how blurry the boundaries of this stuff we call trance are.

Many people, when they first learn this stuff, think it is just like relaxation techniques or guided fantasy, and I agree that many times people who are experiencing those techniques wind up going into trance, but I think there is something different going on in trance, which distinguishes it from those approaches. We'll get into that more as we go along.

This morning we've been through a summary of the basic elements of a solution-oriented induction. For those of you who like step-by-step lists, here's one that might help you get the big picture. I call it the Hitchhiker's Guide to Hypnosis. This is to help remind you not to panic (and bring your towel if you know the literary reference). I could have called it "Tranceland on $5 a Day," but I thought that would be too flippant, and you know what a serious scholar I am.

The Hitchhiker's Guide to Hypnosis

Step 1. *Take off the pressure and validate the person where he/she is and will be.*

Give people permission to feel/think/experience whatever they are and what they might be in the future.

> EXAMPLE: "You can just let yourself be where you are. If you are nervous, that's okay. You don't have to be relaxed to be in trance. You don't have to listen to or believe everything I say."

If they respond in some way or do something that they might think is wrong or distracting, validate it and include it in the trance.

> EXAMPLE: "That's right. You can open your eyes whenever you want and look around. You may want to close them again or just leave them open and stay in trance, whatever is more comfortable for you."

Step 2. *Develop a rhythm.*

Speak only when the person exhales. Even if you skip a breath or two, start speaking again on the exhalation.

Step 3.   Create an expectancy for responding to trance induction and suggestion.

Presume that the person will go into trance and will get the intended results.

EXAMPLE: "I don't know how quickly or deeply you will go into trance. Each person is different" or "You may or may not notice when you first start to relax more and feel more comfortable."

Step 4.   Suggest some automatic changes.

EXAMPLE: "Your hand may start to lift up automatically, just a bit at a time," or "You may be experiencing some numbness in some part of your body. That numbness could increase until you really notice it."

Step 5.   Once you get a response, validate, extend, and direct the change towards the goal.

EXAMPLE: "And as that hand lifts up, you can be going deeper into trance and getting ready to relax even more."

Step 6.   Invite the person out of trance and suggest future positive results.

EXAMPLE: "Now at your own rate and pace, you can come out of that trance and reorient all the way, bringing with you any resource or learnings you need and the ability to go into trance easily and quickly."

I'd like to make one last point before we take a break and move on to the demonstration. I've learned something profound from my practice of therapy in general from doing solution-oriented hypnosis and that is the power of permission and validation in helping people move on.

You know, Transactional Analysis talks about how we sometimes operate out of life scripts and injunctions. Injunctions are ideas like, "You must be perfect," "You'll never be good enough," "It's not okay to be angry," "Big boys don't cry," etc. The idea is that clients take these notions in and act as if they are true until they get unhooked from them. Well, this way of inducing trance sometimes goes a long way towards undoing these injunctions because of its permissiveness. It's a permission that seems to go beyond just intellectually realizing that the injunctions are not necessarily true for you. This approach seems to get the injunctions where they live, in people's unconscious, in their bodies.

I have learned that this inclusive, permissive approach not only takes the pressure off people to perform or "do it right," which can interfere with trance for them, but can be generally therapeutic because it gives them a space, a time, and a relationship where they do not have to be right or are not dominated by their injunctions. Usually, I include a permission to feel or to experience something and a permission not to have to feel or experience anything.

To say to a person, "You can be right where you are, not having to do this any particular way. There is no right or wrong way to go into trance. You can be relaxed if you are relaxed, and you don't have to be relaxed. You can be paying attention to my words, and you don't have to pay attention," can give them a general sense of validation, of "okayness."

I learned this powerfully when I was working with a client who had terribly intrusive obsessions. He was rarely, if ever, free of them. He had seen a psychoanalytic expert on obsessive-compulsive disorders for some time, who pronounced the client the worst case of obsessiveness he had ever seen. I used hypnosis with the man and, by the second session, he was starting to develop fine trances.

At the third session, I started the trance induction with my usual sort of spiel, "You can be where you are, feeling what you are feeling, thinking what you are thinking, obsessing what you are obsessing about, and experiencing what you are experiencing. There's nothing to do to go into trance, no right way or wrong way to go into trance. So just let yourself be where you are, doing what you are doing, worrying that you won't go into trance." At that point, his eyes popped open and he said simply, "That's why I come here." "To go into trance, you mean?" I asked. "No," he replied, "To hear those words." He later explained that it was the only time in his life when he could escape from the terrible sense that he was constantly doing his life incorrectly. He would also often be obsession-free during parts of the trance.

This sense of validation and nonjudgment is, in part, what attracted me to Erickson's hypnotic work. Hypnosis is often seen as manipulative. Used respectfully, I think it is the exact opposite. It is empowering and can free people from manipulation.

TWO

Demonstration, Exercises, and Examples of Induction

NOW THAT YOU HAVE HEARD some examples and learned the elements, it is time to do a demonstration for you. This will put all these elements together, because right now it might seem to you like a book that my friend, Jim Wilk, saw in a golf pro shop that was called *365 Things to Remember About Your Golf Swing*. The purpose of the exercises and demonstrations that will follow is for you to begin to put these elements together in a seamless way. Later you can add the artistry and the poetry. Tomorrow we will add the direction and therapeutic techniques.

What I'd like is to have somebody come up on this chair who would like to experience trance. That could be either somebody who has never experienced trance before and is curious and interested to find out what that experience would be or somebody who has been in trance before.

Demonstration #1: Basic Induction

(*Dennis has volunteered.*)

BILL: Okay. Now the first question I have for you is: Have you ever been in one of these formal trances before?
DENNIS: Yes.

BILL: A fair amount, a few times?

DENNIS: A few times.

BILL: Do you wear contact lenses?

DENNIS: No.

Just a technical note, usually with the advances in contact lenses, people can keep them in while you do trance, but occasionally people have the old kind or for one reason or another, they may want to remove them. It's probably a good idea to give them the option of removing them, blinking often enough, or keeping their eyes open if they wear the contacts.

BILL: Okay. So when you have been in trance before, has it usually been sitting in a chair, has it usually been eyes closed or eyes open?

DENNIS: Sitting in a chair usually—eyes closed.

BILL: Eyes closed usually. And have you ever had any of those trance phenomena experiences, like hand levitation or arm levitation or amnesia or time distortion or glove anesthesia or anything like that?

DENNIS: Amnesia, I thought . . .

BILL: You thought you had it but you forgot. (*Laughter*)

DENNIS: Maybe hand levitation, I can't remember . . . (*Laughter*)

BILL: Okay. Possibly hand levitation. All right, so you don't really know. Good. I suppose the best way to start is exactly like that with your arms uncrossed and your legs uncrossed. And I usually tell people that, not because they *have* to do that, because you can go into a trance in any sort of way, but if you keep your legs crossed or whatever, then sometimes your leg falls asleep while you are in trance, okay? So I guess if you are going to close your eyes, you might as well do that now, and for me to remind you that there is no particular right way or wrong way for you to **go into trance** . . . and that your job . . . is just to do whatever you do, experience whatever you experience . . . and to include in your experience anything that might have been a distraction, resistance,

or difficulty . . . so that you can in your own way, find your own
way into trance. Each person's trance is as unique as their finger-
prints . . . and each trance of yours is unique . . . **that's right** . . .
making whatever adjustments you need as you go along for your
comfort . . . physical adjustments . . . psychological adjustments
. . . emotional adjustments . . . so that you can consciously include whatever you need to include in terms of your thoughts,
your feelings, your sensations, you might be distracted by sounds
around . . . distracted by your own thoughts . . . so that your unconscious mind can create a trance experience for you that's appropriate for you and remember to give yourself permission to **respond**
as you **respond** and to validate yourself for those responses and
you don't have to **go into trance** any **deeper** than is appropriate for
you right now. So you can allow yourself to **go into** the kind of
trance that's right for you . . . and consciously at first you can
include the thought that you might not **go into the trance that you
want** or that you might be trying so hard that it's getting in the
way. So there is nothing in particular that you need to do to **go
into trance** . . . and you might be **going deeper** as time goes on or
you might find yourself **going deeper** then coming out a little, then
going in even deeper, coming out a bit more and going back in. Or
you just might find yourself staying exactly at that level, having
that be **comfortable** for you, I don't really know. . . . Sometimes
when people are in trance, and they appear to be **comfortable** from
the outside and they tell me later that their heart was beating,
that they were feeling a little un**comfortable**, so if either of that's
happening you can include that in your trance experience . . . and
what can you experience in trance? . . . what you have experienced
in trance before or something different. I feel something **changing
in my perceptions** as I **go deeper into trance.** In trance you might
change time. When I was a kid, I went to catholic school and it
was a fairly oppressive atmosphere . . . and I couldn't wait to get
out of class every day at 3:00 every day. And it always seemed to
me that last half an hour, from 2:30 until 3:00, was the longest
half hour of the day, especially since we had an industrial clock in
the front of the classroom on which the **hands** would stick on a
certain number for what seemed like, to that boy sitting in the
desk, hours and hours, but what was probably only a few minutes

of clock time. So what I didn't realize at the time was that I was learning a lot that would do some good for me later when I wanted to use time distortion in hypnosis . . . that watching those **hands** stick on the 6 and then jump up three minutes and stick on the 2:33 and then **jump up** another minute in a few seconds, I was learning how to **change time**, expand time so that I had all the time that I needed in trance to have the experiences . . . that I wanted to have in trance. I was also learning how to divide my attention, because one part of my mind was on the clock in the front of the room, one part of my mind was on what was going on in the classroom, the teaching, the activity, and another part of my mind was anticipating what I was going to do after I got out of class. Just the freedom and the play that I'd experience. So in trance, you can **change time** to make sure that you have all the subjective time that you need that's different from clock time. Because calendar time and clock time are different. When I was flying back from Australia last year, the captain came on the intercom and said, "In two minutes it will be yesterday. If you didn't like the Easter you had this year, you can have another one." So calendar time is different from internal time. Clock time is different from internal time and you can have all the time that you need in there . . . now you talked before about that experience of **hand** levitation, **arm** levitation. And I think that earlier on in our lives we learn to **move** in a different way from the conscious ways we learn to **move** later . . . as a child, as an infant . . . if you've ever observed infants, they **move** their **hands** in sort of jerkier spasmodic ways and the research indicates they don't even know when a **hand** flashes in front of their **face** that that **hand** belongs to them . . . 'cause they don't have a sense of differentiation yet, they don't make that distinction. So the **hand** flashes in front of their **face** and after a while they get that it's correlated, that a certain feeling inside their body and pretty soon . . . they learn to reach for things. So those earlier experiences of **movement** can be the seeds for that automatic **lifting**, that becomes **hand** levitation, **arm** levitation where that **hand** starts to **lift on it's own**, but the conscious mind really doesn't have to levitate it. **That's right**, and usually what I suggest is that it **lift up to your face**, it doesn't have to, but it could **lift up to your face on its own**. And you consciously could be monitoring that or

noticing that or you could be drifting off into your own thoughts
or experiences somewhere else and **that hand could continue** and
the **arm can continue to lift up towards your face** and usually I
suggest that that becomes linked to something you'd like to experience. As that **hand lifts up, arm lifts up** and as it touches your **face**,
or as it's **lifting up off your thigh to your face** it can be linked to be
working on some issue you've wanted to work on, getting a new
perspective on things, that you've wanted to see from a new perspective . . . creating a little more choice in there about some area
you would like to have a little more choice about or just learning
to **go deeper** as the hand and **arm lifts up** in its own way, of its
own rate and of its own pace . . . and will it **lift all the way to the
face**, I don't really know . . . and maybe you don't really know
consciously, but your body knows, your unconscious mind knows,
how much further it will **lift up**. Sometimes there's that old expression that the right hand doesn't know what the left hand is doing.
So it could be that . . . and what you discover is that the **left hand**
starts to **lift** as well and it doesn't have to, it's just a possibility.
And sometimes, what people find is the hands start to have sort of
a race up to their **face**, I think that's interesting to experience to
find out the rate at which the hands move up, 'cause I always figure
if you are gonna have competition with yourself you might as well
set it up so that you win either way. So whichever hand wins, you
win by having the trance **learning**, the trance experience, or if it's
just that right hand that continues to **lift up**, that you can have an
experience that you want in trance. And I can give you another
invitation in trance, and the invitation is to have one or both of
your **hands go numb**, which they call glove anesthesia in hypnosis.
Glove anesthesia is as if you put on a glove that carries within
it topical anesthetic that makes the hand feel **cool** or **numb** or
disassociated just detached . . . because when you have that hand
and arm levitation can be a little **disarming** at first till you learn to
feel comfortable with it or just detach from it. So I can reach over
and touch one of your hands lightly and you may feel the touch or
you may not feel the touch . . . but the aftereffects of that touch
can turn into a **numbness** or **coolness** that might actually happen
in the other hand surprisingly or it might have already happened in
one or both of the hands. As that hand continues **up towards your**

face, learning even more about your ability to respond and trust yourself at the deeper levels, the unconscious level, and be more freed up to work with yourself instead of against yourself. More aligned consciously and unconsciously—like you're lining up all the tumblers in a lock and things just become aligned in a way that the lock goes open and do you know where those hands are right now? . . . and do you know how much farther the hands will move, how much more? And your attention can be divided between what it is that you want to experience, what it is that you are experiencing and distractions. That those main experiences and you can validate yourself for the responses that you make . . . that's right . . . responding in a way that is really right for you . . . to the level that's right for you . . . to help you face things in a different way, to have your unconscious help you move towards goals . . . when I ride in airplanes I go into my travel trance . . . put on my music and I read or I write . . . the next thing I know I'm at my destination. I can just learn to pull into my cocoon, take care of myself in various ways and act appropriately, it's like driving to work with the same route everyday . . . you know that you got there somehow but you didn't recognize all the scenery all of the time and you didn't remember turning on your blinker going into another lane, but somehow you have a vague memory that you must have done that right because you seem to have gotten to work in one piece, feeling pretty comfortable not having noticed what you have done, where you have been. Now because of our time frame, what I suggest is that you take about another minute or two of clock time, as much internal subjective time as you need to complete your experience in trance today . . . and that probably will mean allowing those hands to drift back down to your thighs or placing them down there deliberately, whatever is right for you and starting the process of reorientation to the present time and the present place. Remembering you sitting in your body in a chair in this particular room, at this particular time and when you're ready, as that hand or those hands touch your thighs or legs, that's right, you can start to begin the process of reorientation. When you are ready to come all the way out of trance you can put yourself all the way back together, open your eyes and come all the way out. . . . Good, okay. Pilot to co-pilot. How was that?

DENNIS: It was good.

Let's open it up to a few questions and comments from the peanut gallery here and find out what they have to say. Questions or comments about what you observed?

AUDIENCE: Do you always stretch and yawn when you are done?

Usually. It's a contextual cue saying, "Hey, this hypnosis stuff is over. We are having a different conversation now. Reorient to your body; I'm going to reorient to mine." I'm moving around, touching my body. That's what people usually do when they reorient from a trance, so I give the cue to come out of a trance nonverbally as well as verbally. There's another purpose for my body stretching. While doing trance with the person, I've also been in trance. So I reorient myself to my body as a way of coming out of that trance. Other questions or comments?

AUDIENCE: How come we all didn't go into trance when you were doing this?

Some people did and some people didn't. My induction is just an invitation, it's not a demand, so some people will take me up on the invitation, will ride on the demonstration trance, and some won't. As the days go on though, I think more and more people will ride on it as they get more experience and trust of the process. I think some people at this point are probably freaked out about the process of trance. I'm not certain, but having done other seminars and talked to enough people, they are still thinking at this point, "I don't want anybody to control me, I don't want anybody to make me cluck like a chicken" and stuff like that. They really have weird ideas, like the idea that trance can control people. Once they get more trust with themselves in the process they are more willing to take a risk, but it's okay with me if they do and it's okay with me if they don't.

This induction was mainly oriented towards Dennis and whoever could ride on it could ride on it. But I wasn't oriented towards

them. If you were in front of me and you were having some concerns or objections, hopefully you would be coaching me to include
what I need to include for you rather than for Dennis, because I
was mainly speaking to Dennis's experiences during that demonstration. If you and Dennis were up here it would have been more
likely that both of you would have gone into trance, even if you
hadn't gone in while sitting there. Because I would be aiming it a
little more at your experience and to what you were teaching me
was working for you. You would be teaching me that by giving me
some sort of responses, your hand would be moving or not, you
would be frowning or nodding or you wouldn't be nodding. You
would be breathing differently, so your coaching would have influenced what was happening up here.

AUDIENCE: I noticed that when you were talking about
hand movements I went to my face to scratch and I didn't
really mean to, and I looked around the room and a lot of
people were moving their hands.

Sure. That could be from just sitting and watching something
for a while, people *do* fidget a little; but it could have been influenced by what I was saying.

AUDIENCE: Were you in a trance?

Yes, of course. I've been in a trance all day, haven't you noticed?
I was in a different kind of trance here—very much focused on
Dennis. An externally focused trance. Now if *he* were going to put
me in a trance, I usually have my glasses off and my eyes would
have been closed and I would have looked much more like he
did. I was in an externally focused trance, narrowing my focus of
attention. I wasn't really much noticing you folks out there. I was
much more focused on him and my facial muscles flattened out a
bit and my speech was different than it is right now. So, yes, I was
in a trance.

Hopefully this demonstration had something to do with what
I taught this morning. I wasn't really paying attention to doing
everything I taught, I just do it on automatic pilot. Hopefully you

were able to see and hear some of the elements that we talked
about.

AUDIENCE: I noticed your breathing was mimicking and
mirroring his, and as he exhaled you spoke.

That's right, except at certain special times, which I'll talk about
later. I was keeping time with the movement of my head as well. I
did the conscious and the unconscious dissociation a bit.

AUDIENCE: It seems like you were using confusion technique, there was a lot you were saying, and it had the effect
for me of creating some confusion.

Yes, it was a little hard to follow sometimes, partly because my
phrases were broken up because I stopped talking when he stopped
exhaling and I started talking when he exhaled again. So that's a
little hard to follow logically and linearly, that can be somewhat
confusing. But in general, I don't favor using confusion. I find it to
be a bit disrespectful and tricky.

AUDIENCE: And you were mirroring his body postures.

A lot, yes.

AUDIENCE: When Dennis's eyes closed he couldn't see
that, so is that more for you than it was for Dennis?

Well, he can hear the distinctions; he can hear the differences.
Even if he doesn't process it consciously I think he can hear it at
some level, so even with his eyes closed tonal distinctions are very
powerful, spatial location ones are fairly powerful as well. When I
said **lift up** . . . that gets communicated even with his eyes closed
in the process. Any questions or comments from you, Dennis? Did
you experience the numbness in your hand?

DENNIS: I wasn't sure I felt you touch my hand.

Okay, one more question.

AUDIENCE: You seem to offer more experiences from your own personal background rather than to offer choices for him to experience. Is there any difference?

Telling personal stories is just one of the ways to offer possibilities. I didn't say you have to experience what I experienced, I was trying to evoke something from his experience by telling something from mine, which is typical in storytelling. You just tell stories about yourself and people will either ride on those experiences or they won't. So, yeah, I told some of my experiences as possibilities for him to create his own experience. My guess is that some of you out there and maybe you, Dennis, when I was talking about me being in a classroom, you were in your classroom, you were seeing your clocks, sitting in your desks. I didn't say, "Go sit in a desk," I didn't say, "Go visualize a desk or a clock" or "Go be in school," I just was telling my experience. But usually, when you tell your experience in a evocative enough way, other people will ride on it. But if you say, "Visualize a classroom," some people say, "Oh, I don't visualize well" or "I'm not doing this right," so I wanted to make it more of an indirect possibility. One of the ways to offer multiple choice options is telling stories, which we'll be getting into as we go along.

AUDIENCE: Was that just a random selection of stories?

No, it was not a random selection. It was a very purposeful selection of stories. It was somewhat derived from associations, that is, one story would associate to another, but there was a sequence of suggestions and ideas and possibilities that I was giving. The first set of stories were about going into trance, the second set was about creating changes in perceptions, and the third set of anecdotes had to do with creating changes in muscular movements. Then there were a few others, but that was the sequence as I remember it right now.

All right, thank you for being up here, Dennis.

What we've done this morning is to bring you through the basics of the elements of Ericksonian induction, play you a few examples on the tape recorder and hear how different people do it: Erickson and myself, so far. We've also had this live demonstration so you could get a sense of how to put all those elements together. What we'll do this afternoon is start you practicing one little piece of each element of Ericksonian induction at a time. I'll do another demonstration this afternoon. We'll play a little more audio and videotape this afternoon. We'll add a little more didactic material mainly on trance phenomenon, hypnotic phenomenon—anesthesia, hand levitation, and things like that—so you can understand why would you ever use those, what they are about, and how you elicit them. We'll have some practice on that as well.

Again, all this is leading towards tomorrow, which will answer the question, "What do you do once you get 'em into trance?" The stuff that we do today is going to be relevant for what we talk about tomorrow, and there are going to be pieces of what we do today that we are going to expand on tomorrow. So, even if you've already had a background on Ericksonian hypnosis, don't worry if some of this is repetition for you. Today we're building the background for tomorrow's teaching because the main point is using this stuff in therapy for results. I think inducing a trance is fairly simple, and I think you can learn that fairly quickly. What to do once you get them into trance is a much more complex matter and I think needs much more clarity.

So far, I think you're with me in getting a clearer understanding, I'm seeing enough head nods, and you are laughing in the right places so I have a good sense that you are getting it. This afternoon we are going to ask you to do some work. This is a *work*shop. The work is doing these exercises but I will make them the least threatening that I can make them. I'm still going to ask you to do some work and to take some risks, okay?

Okay, so now I expect you all to do some trances that are just like that demonstration I just did. (*laughter*) Just kidding. I promised I'd walk you through this one step at a time and I will.

For the anxious among you, I have prepared a crib sheet or cheat sheet that you can hang on to and use in preparing for or doing hypnosis during these two days or back in your practices.

Handout 2.1

WORDSMITHING IN SOLUTION-ORIENTED HYPNOSIS

1. Use possibility, permission, and empowering words and phrases.
   "Feel free to tune out anything that I say that doesn't fit for you."
   "You can just let yourself respond in whatever way you do and validate that response."

2. Use inclusive language and phrases.
   "You can be distracted as you go into an altered state or you might be focused on just what I say or you might be concentrating in a relaxed way."
   "You don't have to be relaxed and you can relax."

3. Make distinctions (splitting).
   "You can distinguish between the things that you did and the things that were done to you."
   "One part of you can be paying attention to the sounds and another can pay attention to the sounds inside."

4. Attribute resistance, distractions, skepticism, and analysis to the conscious mind and automatic experience and ability to the unconscious.
   "Your conscious mind may be thinking that you can't go deeply into an altered state and at the same time your unconscious mind is beginning the process of going deeper inside."

5. Propose linkages and associations (linking).
   "As that hand lifts up to your face, you can use that as a signal that your unconscious mind and your body are working together to help you move towards your goals."
   "And in the future, when you need it, your unconscious can give you access to the resources you need to solve your difficulties."

6. Encourage desired responses and include potentially troublesome ones.
   "That's right, the hand can just continue to lift at its own rate and pace."
   "And you can make whatever adjustments you need to maintain and deepen a sense of comfort in trance, even if you are not relaxed."
   "You can open your eyes, as you just did, and still be internally focused. They might close or remain open . . . I don't know what will be right for you."

(continued)

Handout 2.1

CONTINUED

7. Presuppose certain responses and then speculate as to how and when the responses will occur.
   "I don't know how quickly that hand will lift up to your face."
   "I don't know exactly what you'll accomplish when you are inside. Perhaps you won't even be able to tell for sure until after you come out."

8. Use words that are unspecified as to person, place, time, thing, or action. Use outline words for which the client has to provide much of the specific meaning.
   "There are lots of learnings that you have had in the past that you have consciously forgotten about."
   "You can draw upon experiences, wishes, hopes, dreams, skills, abilities, and anything else you need to accomplish your goals."
   "You can go to a certain time and certain place to get what you need; it might be a time in the past or a time in the future; it might be nearby or far away."

Some people like to have these things to hold on to or refer back to and others of you would rather just get it by osmosis. Either way, I expect you to eventually go beyond my style and my ideas and make these methods and techniques your own—fit them into your own practice and models of therapy.

So here is the handout. I have given you a number of categories and then included a few examples of each category. When you do your exercises, you can use these phrases verbatim or use them as models to generate your own similar phrases.

Videotape Example #1: Milton Erickson — Induction by Evocation

Now this next segment is a lot more challenging, it's from the late 50s, and Erickson is working with a guy who's never been in trance before except for a brief experience the night before at a party. It seems that Erickson did a brief trance induction with him during the previous evening at a social gathering. They are sitting in the same room where the party has been the night before and there are people behind a one-way mirror watching and somebody is in the room recording them for research purposes (I believe Gregory Bateson is running the camera, but it's unclear).

This guy has never formally been in a trance before, and you hear Erickson first making a little chitchat with him about the one-way mirror and sort of chiding the people behind the mirror about the supposed neutrality of their one-way mirror because Andre Weitzenhoffer lights a cigarette and you can see through the mirror. Erickson's saying, "I wonder about the one-way mirrors that they use, and I wonder if they realize that you can betray yourself through the one-way mirror." He's commenting on the supposed neutrality of their research and realizing that they are having an influence on people by having the one-way mirror. He starts to idly chitchat and then, as he starts to focus in, you can hear his voice change, see his posture change, his demeanor, and what does he do? He initially reorients this guy to the night before where he was talking to him about trance.

ERICKSON: I wonder if Andre realizes that you can . . . see that. And I wonder about the experimental work that they do here. Whether they're aware that they can betray themselves through the one-way mirror. Do you remember the first time we met?

SUBJECT: Yes.

ERICKSON: You were sitting not quite in that position. I was over on your left side, isn't that right?

SUBJECT: That's right. On my *right* side.

ERICKSON: And . . . that's right, on your *right* side. And, let's see, there's Hilgard over slightly to the left of the room in the same general relative position where Bateson is right now.

SUBJECT: Uh huh.

ERICKSON: And I don't remember where any of the others were, but they were scattered around and they were rather silent as they listened to what I had to say to you. And one of the things I mentioned to you was this matter of feeling yourself, do you recall?

SUBJECT: Yes, I remember, yes.

He's re-evoking the previous evening: "Do you remember the first time we met?" and he makes a mistake, and the guy corrects him, but he keeps re-evoking.

ERICKSON: And as you remember that, do you remember just what happened to you as you recalled it?

Okay, so he says, "and I mentioned this matter of *feeling* yourself"—he tries to stretch out his voice, a little change in his demeanor, and he says, "and as you recall that [*linking*] do you recall . . . "—to link one experience to another.

ERICKSON: You felt yourself doing what? That's right, you felt yourself going into a trance as you'll recall; just as you're going into a trance right now.

The guy starts to respond. "You felt yourself doing what?" and the guy starts to flatten out his facial muscles, change his breathing, he gets very immobile. Erickson responds to these changes by saying, "That right, going into a trance. Just as you are going into a trance right now." Erickson's head is nodding in time to his breathing.

ERICKSON: And I'd like to have you feel yourself in a different position.

Erickson gets directive once he gets an initial response.

Exercise #1: Induction With Permission and Splitting

I'd like you to do an exercise so you can start to get these skills into your behavior. For these first couple of exercises you don't have to put people into trance. You're just going to talk the talk and walk the walk of trance induction. While I say that, though, some people may go into trance as you are doing these exercises—some people may already be experienced.

There's going to be one element that will be consistent throughout all the exercises we will do. Now you don't have to do it in your office in the future, but I'm going to ask that you do it in this setting, and that is, that you **speak only when the person exhales.** How can you notice when people exhale? If you haven't been making this distinction, then I suggest that you just watch my shoulders when I breathe. What happens with my shoulders when I inhale and exhale? They go up and down slightly. Or, find some part of their clothing that moves in response to or along with their breathing. Speak only when they are exhaling. Even if it means that you skip a couple of breaths, as long as you come in on the exhale. Even if it means that you break up your sentences and even stop in the middle of a sentence or a phrase. You are going to wait for that exhalation and speak only then and stop as soon as they stop exhaling. That's the first element and it's going to be the common element as we add others.

The next element for this first exercise is **give them permission to experience whatever they are experiencing** (feel, think, whatever). Give them basic permission and validation for whatever response that they give.

The third element in this first exercise is **start to create this conscious/unconscious split.** You can do it verbally and nonverbally. What I usually do, and this is a recommendation, is to attribute all the concerns, resistances, and distractions to the conscious mind, and attribute trance to the unconscious mind and automatic experience to the unconscious mind: "Your *conscious* mind may be distracted by the sounds around, by the other people talking. Your *conscious* mind may be wondering whether you can go into a trance." All the skepticism, all the worries and concerns, I usually attribute to the conscious mind: "And your *unconscious* mind at the same time can be remembering all the previous trance-like experiences. Your *unconscious* mind may be sure that you can go into a trance while your *conscious* mind may be sure that you can't go into a trance. Your *unconscious* mind can be helping you experience whatever you need to experience in the way that is right for you." Just start to make the distinction between the conscious and the unconscious minds.

Also, I usually attribute to the conscious aspects the external,

here-and-now focus of attention. When I go over to the unconscious, I talk about any time other than the now time (the past or
the future) and I talk about any place other than here. Like Erickson was doing with this guy in the last example, when he said, "I'd
like you to feel yourself in a different location," and he has him
remember back to the previous evening, so he does both the distinctions of having the guy go back in time to the previous night and
having him change his position as well and feel himself in a different position. You can do all those in addition, if you want, but the
main one I want you to get in here is speaking on the exhale, giving
the person permission to respond however they do, and make the
conscious and unconscious distinction both verbally and nonverbally.

Your job in these exercises is to feel awkward, feel as if you
can't do it and make a lot of mistakes. Do you think you can do
that? Because the point is if this isn't your usual way of working in
therapy, that has got to be a bit awkward when you start. However, we are going to break it up in little pieces so it gets less
awkward as you go along. We are going to give you enough model-
ing and practice so that by osmosis at the end of the two days, it
will be very much less awkward and more comfortable. All right?
Just take about five or six minutes and go both ways and switch
after about five minutes and have the other person be the talker.
One talker, one listener. This isn't hypnotist and subject, just talk-
ers and listeners at this point. I'll give you a halfway time signal.

(*Participants do the exercise.*)

Actually, when I go to workshops I hate to do exercises, and I
always get value out of doing them. This workshop has a lot of
exercises so you will be a lot more confident about using trance in
your practice.

Questions or comments, what did you learn by doing that?

AUDIENCE: Is it okay to speak on the inhale all the time?

Sure. If you choose a particular pattern and that works for you,
that's fine as long as you keep it and develop it as an automatic

pilot pattern. The other thing I can say, though, is if you already have a pattern developed where you do a lot of relaxation training or a lot of guided fantasy or a lot of biofeedback kind of things or autogenic training, please leave that pattern at the door. You can have it back when you leave. I assume you are already good at that. What I'd like you to do is get *these* automatic patterns, and then you can put the two together when you leave. If speaking on the inhale, then, is one of your old patterns, you might develop more flexibility and speak on the exhale, but if speaking on the inhale feels more comfortable for you, and you haven't had a particular pattern before, fine.

AUDIENCE: Yeah, I could do it any which way? I was just wondering.

No, there's nothing magical about it.

AUDIENCE: When you are talking, you are exhaling, I guess, and it does keep your breathing together.

Yes, it does keep your breathing together, but it's not essential. It's not essential to speak on that kind of rhythm, but I think it's nice. The other thing I say is when I ask for hand levitation, I ask for it on the inhale. I use it for that as a specific purpose, and we'll be talking about that later. Okay, so what else?

AUDIENCE: I felt very disjointed or uncomfortable.

In listening or in talking?

AUDIENCE: In talking.

To a certain extent that's a function of the exercise, because you haven't got a lot of content to put in there yet. Also, it's a little awkward and not your usual way to talk, but as we go along we'll give you more content and it will get easier. You will have a few more examples as well, both audio and videotape demonstrations.

AUDIENCE: As soon as she closed her eyes, I felt more comfortable.

Aha. That certainly was true for me when I first started. We are going to have exercises you do where the person keeps their eyes open as they go into trance, but at first for me it was like "close your eyes, I don't want your fish eyes looking at me while I'm doing this, because I feel a little awkward about this whole thing." Now sometimes I do trance having the person keep their eyes open. We'll talk about that as we go along and have you do more exercises, again, as you get more comfortable. We'll have some exercises where the person talks as well. For now, though, we are just having you talk to them.

AUDIENCE: I just found it a little hard to attend to everything at once. I felt like I needed to be looking at them in the eyes and then trying to notice when they were breathing.

That's a little difficult sometimes, so usually what I'll do is notice their breathing with my peripheral vision, out of the corner of my eye. I keep that eye contact and I keep my head moving in time with the breathing. So that's one way to do it, but again, you could not look them in the eye.

Audiotape Example #2: Milton Erickson — Induction With Permission and Splitting

Okay, let's add another example before you do another exercise. This is the first time the guy's been in trance, he's learning about hypnosis. He's a photographer who has an artistic block. You can hear the conscious/unconscious dissociation and presumably it will be more meaningful now that you've just done it.

Even though you may be intensely interested consciously, I would like to have you appreciate the fact that you are infinitely more interested at an unconscious level. And consciously you can just relax; you can close your eyes and let your mind wander at will, from my words, to thoughts of photography, to thoughts of Dr. Herschman, to thoughts of the weather, to thoughts of your daily work, to thoughts of what you had for breakfast today — any wandering thought that comes to your mind. There should be no effort on your part to try to listen to me, no effort whatsoever. Just as you watch a flower open, you can sit and watch it without making any effort of your own. In exactly the same way, you can let your unconscious mind open and do its own thinking, its own feeling, without any effort whatsoever on your part. All you need to know is that your unconscious mind does exist; it is within you. It is a part of you that you do not really know and never really will know, but which knows a tremendous amount about you.

Okay, now that you've actually done that exercise, you can hear that Erickson was making the conscious and unconscious dissociation. He was also giving a lot of permission for distraction, for wandering thoughts, and he was attributing some things to the conscious mind and other things to the unconscious mind. The unconscious mind, he was implying, has a lot of knowledge and a lot of power and the conscious mind has only a limited sort of power.

Now go back to the Using Presupposition in Hypnosis handout (1.2, p. 18). That will help you in the next exercise.

Now to the next piece. The next piece is the use of presupposition. You've got this handout as a guide. I'd like you to have some experience using presupposition in trance induction. Again, the first step is the same as before — speak on the exhale. Next, imply or presuppose that the person is going to go into trance. Or, after you see some response, presume that they have gone into trance. Then, the third step in this exercise is to speculate aloud with them about the varied experience they could have while going into trance. The key here is never to doubt that they are going to go into trance, only to speculate about all the ways that they could accomplish that. They might be distracted, their conscious mind might not believe they are going into trance, as they are going into trance.

You can use this sheet of ways to presuppose as your cheat

sheet. You can have it on your lap and look at it and say, "Would you like to go into trance now or later?" rotely following it, or you can get a little more creative by looking down at this and making up new sentences, new questions. You can use this technique using questions or statements, so it might be, "Would you like to go into trance with your eyes open or your eyes closed?" or it might be the statement, "Some people like to go into trance with their eyes open, some people like to go into trance with their eyes closed. I really don't know which would be most comfortable for you or which you would like." The latter is a statement rather than a question.

You are going to imply and presuppose the person's going into trance, never doubt that, Erickson's got that handled, he's behind you, I've got that handled, I'm behind you, we are going to put the person into trance, you don't have to worry about it, it's going to happen. All you are going to have to do is speculate aloud to them on the process of going into trance, what they'll be aware of, what they will experience and how they'll go into trance. Never question the idea that they are going to go into trance. Does that make sense? All right. Again, one talker, one listener and switch places halfway. Again, they don't have to go into trance, but you are just going to talk about going into trance. The *next* exercise will be about having them go into trance. We are learning to talk this kind of talk and put some of these skills together. You can use whatever you used in the last exercise. You can do the conscious/unconscious dissociation if you want, give them permission, whatever else you want, that's fine as long as you get these new pieces in.

Let me give you a couple of examples before you go. I'm just going to ask Glenn, "Have you ever been in trance *before*"—that's going to be my first presupposition. Now, "Would you like to go into trance with your glasses on or would you like to take your glasses off to go into trance?" Then, "As you take your glasses off, would you like to close your eyes to go into trance, or would you like to keep your eyes open while you are going into trance?" Close your eyes? Okay, "You can do that now" (remember permission from the exercise before). "And as you close your eyes, I wonder how quickly you'll realize that you're going into trance? I wonder what the first sign that you see will be, or the first sign that you feel will be that you are going into trance? And I really don't know how deeply you are going into trance, or how profoundly you are going into trance. I do know that you could have a lot of experiences while you are in trance and that they should be personal experiences for you, not particularly anybody else's experience, but your own experience, at your own rate and at your own pace. So don't go in any more deeply than is appropriate for you. And I really don't know how deeply that is, but I do know that you could have your own trance and experience that in a way that is right for you." Okay, that's fine. Thanks, Glenn.

Just speculate about what kind of trance he's going to experience, never question that he's going to have a trance experience. This exercise doesn't have to take too long. Again, because the point for this exercise is not particularly to get the person into trance, but just for you to learn to talk the talk with the person right in front of you responding. Okay, five or six minutes apiece, first as a talker and then as a listener. Just to reduce your anxiety level I won't be listening to you now, but during the next few exercises I'll be around to coach, and we'll do some other public exercises as well.

(*The participants do the exercise.*)

Start to finish up and come back into the big group. All right, what questions or comments did you have and what learning did you have there?

AUDIENCE: I'm having difficulty being with my own breathing and his breathing, too.

Okay, so you had difficulty noticing his breathing and speaking or paying attention to both at the same time or what?

AUDIENCE: I guess just paying attention. I'm not sure.

Okay, well I think if you are having trouble paying attention to both at the same time, just go in and out of one and the other. At times pay attention to the breathing and at times pay attention to what you are saying, and after a while you'll learn to do both at the same time. It's like riding a bicycle or driving a car at first, you're supposed to look in the rearview mirror, put your hands on the wheel, put the clutch in, put the gas on, and switch gears. It's pretty overwhelming to do all those things at once, so once you get one of them on automatic pilot, you can usually do several of them at the same time. At first driving was pretty overwhelming and now most people can do it in their sleep and as far as I can tell, they do drive in their sleep. (*Laughter*) At first you couldn't do that, you were real tense and nervous and didn't think you'd ever get this and feel comfortable doing it. But obviously after a while, you got comfortable doing it. Okay? What else?

AUDIENCE: One thing that I noticed is, as the listener, I don't hear half of what he says, I mean I'm much more with . . .

It's too bad, I eavesdropped, and what he was saying was very profound. (*Laughter*)

AUDIENCE: My unconscious heard it. (*Laughter*)

Yeah. I've had lots of clients tell me that, and I kid them and say, "I said really profound things and you weren't listening to that?!" Sometimes they just ride on the rhythm of my voice and use the voice as sort of an anchor. They just go away, but link to the voice and that's how they'll know they are supposed to come out. Sometimes they tune in and out of it. This is a very common experience, so obviously it's not just the content of your words that is creating the trance. Maybe you can relax a little about that. After my wife Pat had our baby, she got real real tired. She would do trance with clients and she would occasionally start to fall asleep while she was hypnotizing clients. When she falls asleep while doing hypnosis, she sometimes starts saying totally nonsensical things from images out of her dreams. She said her clients never noticed. She would then wake up and hear what she had just said, and she would try to weave it in in some creative way, but they never really seemed to notice that she was talking this totally nonsensical talk. Maybe that will relax you a bit about the content. What else?

AUDIENCE: Sometimes while doing this I'm trying to imply that he is going to go into trance this way or that way, and he was already into trance.

Then I might say something ambiguous like, "As you're going into a trance. . . . " Now that's not really clearly saying they actually are *now* or whether it's going to be in the future. "As you are going into trance, you might notice the changes in breathing, the changes in blood pressure. . . . "

AUDIENCE: How do you know that they really are in a trance, and you can say, "Now that you are in a trance . . . "?

I watch for common trance indicators. I've given you a list:

flattening of facial muscles

change in skin color

immobility

decrease in orienting movements

catalepsy in a limb

changes in blinking and swallowing

altered breathing and pulse

autonomous motor behavior (jerkiness)

faraway look

fixed gaze

changed voice quality

time lag in response

perseveration of response

literalism

dissociation

relaxed muscles

Find the common trance indicators. Look for a few of these puppies. I would never make it as precise as three out of five or anything, but typically, these are the responses one sees when the person goes into trance.

AUDIENCE: What do you usually see?

What did you see when Dennis came up here that Dennis did differently from the kind of conversations that we usually have with Dennis? First, he doesn't usually close his eyes during a conversation. Sometimes he does, perhaps, but not for that long. So he closed his eyes, and he was breathing in a different way than he usually breathes, his breathing changed. He flattened his facial muscles. If you could see it, he had a slight change in his skin color. He showed immobility—he wasn't moving a great deal.

In this conversation we are having now, most of you are fidgeting around a little, but as soon as we start to have a trance conversation, for some reason, people slow way down and stop moving for the most part. And when they do move, they show that autonomous motor behavior, the jerkiness. They're what's called ideomotor movements in trance, sometimes you can see these little jerky finger movements. Some hypnotists use automatic finger movements as "yes" and "no" signals. In trance, your fingers show a sort of jerky movement.

We also saw changes in blinking and swallowing and catalepsy in a limb. Try to hold your hand up like this for about half an hour or 45 minutes and you'll find that it's very difficult to do it, it gets real heavy or painful or whatever. But Dennis probably had the sense, maybe he didn't, but most people have the sense that their hand is on its own and could stay up there for 15 or 20 minutes, half an hour, even 45 minutes. If you hold it up that long while you're out of trance, after a while it hurts. In trance it doesn't seem to require any effort or hurt. That waxy catatonia you have heard about in psychopathology where you put the person in certain body postures and they stay in that posture is similar. A far away look if their eyes are open, they just sort of stare at one thing and don't move a lot, their eyes are fixed. They have a changed voice quality if they talk and sometimes there's a time lag in their responses, both verbal and nonverbal. Dennis had to wait, I had to wait to see his hand levitation after I invited it. It took a little while. Sometimes you'll ask a question, and you'll think the person didn't hear it, and then they'll answer. It just takes a little while. Also, perseveration of response. Sometimes when you see people nodding in trance, they'll just keep nodding for a long time. Literalism—this is when people really respond exactly very literally, like we used to have this deal when we were learning some of these language skills in our house, and we'd say, "Could you get me a beer?" and the person would say "yes" and wouldn't move. Yeah, I can, it's a possibility.

I rarely have literalism from trance, but occasionally. I remember one person with whom I was doing a trance demonstration in Oxford, England. It was this guy's first time ever in trance. He went into trance, got the arm/hand levitation, lifted it up to his face. Up it went and touched his face. When I wanted him to come out of trance, I said, "and your hand could drift back down to your thigh and as it touches your leg or your thigh you can come all the way out of trance." So down it comes, finally his fingers and hand touch his leg and he opens his eyes, seemingly he comes out of trance, and his hand is touching his leg, but his arm is stuck up in the air. So he looks at me, and I said, "Hello," and he said, "You know, it's weird; my arm just sort of feels sort of stuck here and suspended." I said, "Okay." And he said, "Well, will my arm ever go down?" and I said, "I assume it will eventually." He said, "Well, when?" and I said, "I don't really know," and he asked, "Why didn't it go all the way down when I came out of trance?" I said, "I don't really know." So I said, "Okay, close your eyes and go all the way back into trance." He closed his eyes, went all the way back into trance, and I said, "Now I'll ask your unconscious, why didn't your hand and arm go all the way down?" He replied, "Because you only told my *hand* to go back down to my thigh." So I said, "Picky, picky, picky. Okay, the hand *and* the arm can lift all the way up again and the hand and the hand and arm can go all the back down when you come out of trance." And that was that. They both came down and out he came. But usually you don't get such literalism.

Dissociation is the splitting we talked about, of the person's body from their head. Dissociation of their emotions. Erickson would occasionally have a person remember the humor of their favorite joke and not the intellectual content of it, so they would be laughing and laughing and have no idea what they were laughing about—that's dissociation. Dissociation of emotion from intellect. Dissociation of one part of your body from another part of your body. Dissociation of the conscious from the unconscious mind; any split in your experience that's intense enough for you to notice it. That's usually related to trance. There is not a requirement for any of these things, but these are some of the things to look for.

What I can say is just notice during the next two days when people go into trance, what they do and, all of a sudden, you'll start to get it. More than that, notice what happens for you when you go into trance, and you'll start to get it. A guy came to Erickson and wanted him to define trance, and Erickson wouldn't define it. The guy returned every day and asked Erickson to define trance. Erickson told him he'd only know it by experiencing it. The guy's frustrated and keeps asking Erickson every day, what's trance, what's trance? And Erickson's reply is always, "You'll only know it by experiencing it." He goes out to eat with Erickson, and Erickson's wife pleads with him to tell the guy what trance is because he's making the dinner miserable by his pleading. So Erickson says, "You'll know it when you experience it," and the guy experiences it sometime during the week, and it answers his question. You'll probably have a lot of questions until you figure out "Oh, *this* is trance, I get it," and that's an internal experience. You will also see so many examples of it when you do your exercises, you'll start to say, "I get it—they are in trance."

Exercise #2: Using Analogies and Anecdotes to Induce Trance

Now I want you to do one more exercise before the break and that is evoking trance by **analogy** and **anecdote**. I think there are really four aspects of trance, four doorways into trance.

One of the doorways is spacing out or de-focusing. And there are common, everyday, universal sort of experiences that one could talk about that are common experiences of spacing out or de-focusing. Lying on the grass looking at the clouds. The hypnogogic state, which is when you are just about but not quite asleep state,

Handout 2.2

TRANCEPORTS: THE FOUR DOORWAYS INTO TRANCE

Spacing Out/De-focusing

lying on the grass looking at the clouds
hypnogogic/hypnopompic states
meditating/relaxation states
listening to a boring class/lecture

Absorption/focused awareness

involved in a movie/television/book
listening to a riveting speaker
absorbed in music
absorbed in some activity or work
absorbed in a conversation

Dissociation/splitting of awareness and/or activity

playing an instrument (once you've mastered it)
playing a sport (once you've mastered it)
doodling
eating popcorn in the movies

Rhythmic/pattern/repetitive behavior

chanting
dancing
mantras
running
rocking

and the hypnopompic state, which is the state between sleeping and waking up. Meditating and relaxation states. Listening to a boring class or lecture. Times in natural everyday life when you space out into trance-like states. It's not a formal hypnotic trance but it's trance-like. So that's one of the doorways: spacing out and de-focusing. Not focusing on anything. Sort of spreading your light wide.

The opposite of that is also a characteristic typical of trance and that is **narrowing the spotlight**. The beam of attention is very narrow, like the absorption or focus awareness involved in a movie, television, or book; or listening to a riveting speaker, somebody who really captures your attention; or being absorbed in music.

Sometimes I listen to music and, because I'm a musician, I listen to just one instrument throughout the whole piece of music. I will just, for example, listen to the bass. The rest fades into the background. I'm so absorbed in that—that's a trance. Being absorbed in some activity or work, when you are really into it. Frederick and I were talking about that during one of the breaks. He said, "I think I go into trance sometimes when I do therapy." I said, "You mean, when you are really into it?" and he says, "Yeah, when it's really going smoothly and flowing." Being absorbed in a conversation. Ever have the experience of eating in a restaurant and having dinner with friends of yours and, all of a sudden, you look up and all the waiters and waitresses and the owner are waiting for you to leave? Now for those of you who are nodding, you probably evoked a little of that experience just by me reminding you. That's a common everyday experience of absorption or focus awareness.

Now the next doorway is **dissociation** or splitting of awareness and activity. For example, once you've mastered playing an instrument, you can play it without really thinking about it a lot. If you play the flute, after a while, it just plays itself. You just are sort of there and intending to play something. Sometimes when I play guitar people say, "You are really a good guitar player," and I say, "No, my fingers are, though." By now, I don't know how to play the guitar anymore, but my fingers know really well. If I try to think about it I just get in my own way. This is true of very complicated things especially. Once you've mastered an instrument, if you play it, you are usually doing it in a dissociated way. Playing a sport—same thing. Doing therapy, once you've mastered it. Doing hypnosis, once you've mastered it. You are on automatic pilot and you don't have to think about it. Doodling—a common everyday experience. You are on the phone and you don't even notice what you doodle, you are just doing it. Eating popcorn in the movies, and when your hand hits the bottom you wonder, "Who ate that popcorn?" That's dissociation. Maybe people eat in a dissociated way and don't even recognize what they ate or that they eat, they just eat.

Rhythmic or patterned behavior is the last doorway into trance that I've specified here. That is repeating something in a very rhythmic way, running, rocking, saying mantras, whatever it may be.

Dancing for some people, chanting, those things can be common everyday trance experience. Some people use chanting or mantras to develop a meditation-type trance.

Now these (defocusing, narrowing the spotlight, dissociation, and rhythmic or patterned behavior) are the doorways to trance and you can use common universal experiences that can evoke trance-like experiences. Remember when I was talking about linking earlier. With people, especially those who have never been in trance before, evoke a bunch of trance-like experiences and say, "Now put all those together and this is trance." Grab de-focusing. Grab an experience of focused attention. Grab an experience of dissociation. Grab an experience of rhythmic experience. Here in the front row, you just came back from a trance, welcome back. A common everyday one where you are zoned out for a little while, off in your own experience and then I notice you reorient to your body. You're gone from here for a moment. And I was saying really important stuff, too. (*Laughter*) No, not really. It was all fluff while you were gone.

So, what I'd like you to do for the next exercise before we take a break is to use one of these four doorways or all of the doorways to invite the person into trance, by telling them a bunch of stories about your (and potentially their) experience. So that could be examples of common, everyday trance, and then invite them to use those to go into trance. Again, speak on the exhalation. A second way is to interview the person for any of these common, everyday trance experiences—what ones they have had. Did they play an instrument? Trance-like experiences that are in their experience and background. A third way is to use the experiences they have or universal experiences—ones that most people would have—to evoke trance. Do that by telling stories and using novelistic detail to evoke a memory of those trance-like experiences.

Now what I mean by **novelistic detail** is that, just like a novelist, you try to make the experience come alive for the person. Instead of saying, "The man was sitting in his study," you say, "He was sitting in his study; it was a cold and dark night. He could see the lightning flash every once in a while that illuminated the yard. He could hear the rain against the window pane. He could feel the warmth of the fire against his back. He could hear the scratching of the pen in the quiet of the night between the thunder claps and lightning. He could smell the wood smoke." Now, you've just talked about all the sensory experiences that a person could have in that experience and you've made it a little more novelistic than "sitting in his study, writing." The person can ride on those sensory experiences and get involved in the experience. That's what Garrison Keillor, of Prairie Home Companion fame, does—gives you enough novelistic detail to evoke, but not too much so that it imposes on your experience.

So, give them enough sensory details. Make it alive. That's what I'm learning about writing and teaching. I tell you the general principle, the abstract principle, and then I tell you a story. The story about Pat falling asleep, saying something nonsensical and her clients not noticing, brings the principle of it not mattering exactly what you say during induction alive for you a little. In the same way, what you are going to do is help bring trance alive in the person's experience rather than just telling them about trance.

This time I'd like you to do it only one way and take about ten minutes. One talker/one listener. Before you begin, interview them to find out what common trance experiences they have had. Then do a trance. And be anxious when I come around, okay? Be a little nervous and feel awkward. I'll give you a couple of minutes to get started.

(*Participants do the exercise.*)

All right, what did you experience? What did you learn?

AUDIENCE: It's getting easier.

How so?

AUDIENCE: Some things I didn't have to think about a whole lot, like the breathing. Watching the breathing is a bit more automatic.

Did anyone else feel that about the breathing? I was coaching some people on that as I walked around. What I coached Henry on was the idea of not having to speak on every breath, because his partner Frederick's breathing was fairly rapid. So I'd just speak on every other breath or every third breath. That would slow me down a little. Right now, it seems like a fairly rapid pace for you, so to be able to think about stuff between talking when first learning this is a good thing and also to slow you down a little more and slow him down a little more. What else?

> AUDIENCE: I felt real comfortable and relaxed, except I could see myself in a recliner or another chair being a lot more relaxed. Some people could do it in a sit up chair, I know, but also to add to their experience another chair would be better.

Yes, and I say by the end of this workshop that a lot of your trance will be linked to these straight back chairs and maybe it may be a little harder to do it laying down at that point, because you will have linked so many trances to these chairs. But a recliner may help some people.

> AUDIENCE: I'm a lot more comfortable going into trance than being the one to induce it. (*Laughter*)

Aha, a trance junkie from way back. It takes one to know one, and I'm one so I know. Someone invites me to go into trance and, boom, I'm gone. I find, though, that some people find it a little difficult to get into trance, like there is some struggle going on, a conflict, a lot of mind chatter or whatever. When they do get into trance, though, and I say, "Okay, come out of trance," they say, "Forget you—goodbye, I'm having a great time, I don't want to come back."

> AUDIENCE: One of the things that I noticed as the listener was it really didn't matter what stories Glenn told, 'cause I made up my own. I was really much more aware of what my own experiences were.

That's generally true with Glenn. He tends to just waffle on, and whatever it is he's talking about, that's Glenn, but with other people you'll find that the stories are actually profound. (*Laughter*) Always there with support, right, Glenn? Giving you that basic necessary support, trying to make the learning experience as unthreatening as possible. Someone asked, "How do you get competent in trance?" and I say, "The same way you get to Carnegie Hall—practice, practice, practice." These people know you are not an expert yet, who're you trying to fool, right? So just go for it. I've heard people doing that as I've been going around, so that's pretty good. Good stuff.

THREE

Trance Phenomena:
Getting Your Hands on the
Control Knob of Experience

WHAT WE ARE HEADING INTO this afternoon is a focus on trance phenomena. When hypnosis was first delineated and discovered, in the time of mesmerism, animal magnetism, people found that some subjects that were in trance would spontaneously do some of these trance phenomena:

amnesia—forgetting some specific thing or forgetting being in trance or forgetting their identity

time distortion (contraction or expansion)

age progression—projecting into the future or seeing themselves in the future

age regression—going back into the past

anesthesia—lack of sensation altogether

analgesia—lack of pain.

Early hypnosis investigators found that some or all of these phenomena happened spontaneously for people while in trance.

The handout (3.1) delineates the various trance phenomena.

After a while hypnotists tried to deliberately elicit the trance phenomena as evidence that the person was in trance (this is called ratification) or to get the person deeply absorbed in trance and

Handout 3.1
TRANCE PHENOMENA

MODALITY	+	−
PERCEPTUAL		
External sensory perception	Positive hallucination V/A/T/G/O	Negative hallucination V/A/T/G/O
Internal sensations	New/different sensations	Analgesia/ anesthesia
Orientation in space	Reorientation	Disorientation
MEMORY		
Memory	Hyperamnesia	Amnesia
Orientation in time	Age progression	Age regression
Time flow	Expansion	Contraction
BODY/ PHYSIOLOGY		
Muscle movements	Levitation/ Autom. writing/ ideomotor	Catalepsy
Heart/blood	Increased heart rate/ blood flow	Decreased heart rate/blood flow
Temperature	Warmth/heat	Cool/cold
AFFECT/ ASSOCIATIONS		
Association	New Associations	Dissociation
Affect	New feelings	Losing old feelings

deeper into trance. They were used as deliberate mechanisms for deepening absorption and for ratification. They were used to convince you and the subject that they were in trance. Some of you still have the question, "How do I know that they are in trance and not just sitting there with their eyes closed, breathing?" One of the ways to find out is if you've got **responsiveness**. If the person actually is responding, that's one way to test, if you will, that they are in trance—not the only way, but if they *are* showing responses to what you are saying. So trance phenomena are either internal, subjective sort of experiences or externally observable experiences. They are experiences or behaviors that one can use to check trance and also to get people more deeply involved in trance.

I think one of the things that made Erickson a very hopeful therapist, an optimistic therapist, was that early on he learned hypnosis. What makes you optimistic when you learn hypnosis is you can recognize how people can get their hand on the control knob of experience. I say, "Make your hand numb," and you say, "I don't know how to do that." But if I go through the rigmarole of doing hypnosis and guide you internally, you could make your hand numb. It's nothing you know how to do consciously and deliberately, but it is something that is a possibility for you. So, for some reason, when we put you in trance, you or I could get your hands on the control knob of experience, and I can help you make your hand heat up or cool down or go numb.

Most of us consider our internal experiences as fairly fixed—we feel the way we feel, we sense the way we sense and this is the way it is. For most of us, our physiological processes are pretty much the way they are. In trance, you could put a person in trance, do some dental procedure with them, tell them to bleed a little to clean out the wound and then stop bleeding, and they can do it. Now why and how is that? I don't have a clue, to tell you the truth. All I know is that it seems to work. That is, for some reason, with hypnosis (and there are other ways you could do it, too, hypnosis is just a good way to do it) you can get your hand on the control knob of experience. Erickson learned that early on; he learned that people are pretty changeable. Instead of learning these fixed personality theories that most of us learned to do psychotherapy, he learned a *change* theory. He learned a change technique as well. So he started to explore with people how much they could change their experience of time, of space, of sensation, of their sense of where they were in time, age regression or age progression.

So I've delineated trance phenomena for you in three columns: (see Handout 3.1, p. 78): the left hand column is the person's experience—the modality of human experience or behavior, but usually an internal experience. In the middle column, a plus sign indicates that you are either amplifying or turning up the volume on that particular experience. There is **positive hallucination**, in which you have a person see something, hear something, touch something, taste something, or smell something that isn't there (Visual, auditory, tactile, gustatory, and olfactory). A positive hallucination, then, is something that they see, hear, feel, taste, or smell that isn't really there, but that you add to their sensory experience. Just as you can enhance or amplify, you can turn the volume or intensity down on any of those senses. That would be a **negative hallucination**. Negative hallucination is dropping something out of your experience or diminishing it in your experience. Negative hallucination is when you don't notice something that is in your sensory field.

If you think this is kind of weird stuff, just think about it in terms of everyday life experiences. Some of you may have had the experience of walking around in a crowd and thinking you've heard somebody call you name and turning around and you've found that nobody called your name. Ever had that experience? Then you are either psychotic, or you have had a common, everyday experience of positive hallucination. Many people have had that kind of experience. Maybe you've been in bed and thought you felt a bug but it was just the sheets moving. That's positive hallucination. Adding something to your sensory field that wasn't there. Maybe you've been around somebody who was kind of dirty and you started to itch a lot.

AUDIENCE: Talking about head lice.

Right. Someone talks about head lice and you start to feel all sorts of feelings on your head. Even though logically you know you haven't got lice, you start to get freaked. That's positive hallucination.

How about some common, everyday experiences involving negative hallucination? For those of you who wear glasses, you probably noticed your glasses right when you first got them and then you don't notice them after a couple of days or weeks. It's embarrassing for me because sometimes I look for my glasses when they are on my face. That's really bad. You've dropped something out of your experience. Some people wear watches, wear rings, and they don't notice them after a while if they wear them a lot. I used to be a hippie, so when I first learned to tie a tie to go out and teach workshops, it was like, how do people wear these things? Now I'll get on a plane and get all the way home before I notice I still have my tie on. Negative hallucination. Dropping something out.

You can go all the way down the list, either adding new and different sensations, or dropping some sensations out. Like orientation in space—you can either reorient the person as Erickson was doing with that guy on the tape: "I'd like you to feel yourself in a different position in the room." Or disorientation—not knowing where you are or where some part of your body is in space. Sometimes during hand or arm levitation, people don't know where their arms are, not a clue, they just know the arm is somewhere between their leg and their face. The same thing about memory or time. You can either orient to the future—age progression, turning up the volume, or orient back to the past—age regression, turning down or back the volume. Hyperamnesia is remembering something you haven't remembered very vividly or remembering something you haven't remembered at all—turning up the volume. Amnesia—turning down the volume and not remembering something. Time flow/time expansion, stretching time out subjectively or time condensation or contraction—volume knob down. You can either add automatic movements, automatic handwriting or hand/arm levitation and that ideomotor movement I talked about earlier—the "yes" signals from the fingers; or drop out movement—catalepsy or immobility. Increase heart rate or blood flow, decrease heart rate or blood flow. Add warmth or heat or subtract warmth or heat making it cool or cold. You can add new associations, new linkages or help the person dissociate. In affect we can add new feelings or help diminish the intensity of old feelings or lose old feelings. This is a list of typical things we do in trance, it doesn't cover everything, but it's a pretty good list.

What I want to do now is show you some of these trance phenomena in a demonstration. So three people up here who would like to go into trance—you could have been in trance before or not, either way.

Demonstration #2:
Eliciting Trance Phenomena

BILL: Okay, the question I have for each of you is, have you ever been in one of these formal kind of trances before today?

SUBJECT 1: Sort of, there was someone in my office being put into a trance, and I was there also. I sort of did but I wasn't the subject.

SUBJECT 2: No, never before today.

SUBJECT 3: No, never before today.

BILL: Great, all right. Any questions or comments before you go into trance or particular things you'd liked to do something with while you are in trance, or do you just want to have a profound and interesting experience, or what? You'll take a profound and interesting experience. Okay. Any particular things you'd like to do? Just curious about it? Okay, good. Those of you who wear glasses are welcome to take them off and we'll find a safe place for them or you can put them under the chair or whatever. Okay, good. So I guess the best way to start is to close your eyes **now**. If you don't want to close your eyes, you can keep 'em open, but I might suggest that you find a place to look at on the rug, for example, that might be comfortable for you and just let yourself be exactly the way you are. As I said before, there is nothing particular for you to do to **go into trance** . . . no right way or wrong way to **go into trance**. You can just let yourself consciously be thinking what you are thinking and really not particularly trying to make yourself **go into trance,** 'cause trance is really not a doing, it's more of a not doing . . . more of an allowing. . . . Trance is like going to sleep in that way 'cause it's more of an allowing of sleep to be there rather than making yourself go to sleep. . . . So, consciously, you can let whatever enters your consciousness be there. It could be the distractions or the sounds around, it could be the distraction of knowing that you are sitting up here in front of a group and initially you could be very aware of those things, or you might be attending to your thoughts, wondering whether they are going to **go into a trance** and what it would be like to **go into a trance** . . .

and maybe you'll be wondering how you'll know when you are in a trance . . . so you can just let those thoughts, that wondering on be there and make sure that you take care of yourself in whatever way is appropriate **as you go into trance**. And that you don't **go into trance** any **deeper** than is appropriate for you, right here and right now, or don't **go into a trance** any way that doesn't seem appropriate, right here in front of a group. . . . So you don't really have to do anything to **go into a trance**. . . . You can just allow yourself to have whatever experience you are going to have. It's my job to create the climate for you to go into trance . . . and to be able to include whatever needs to be included . . . in order to facilitate you going into trance. Now much of the time people find they **relax** when they go into trance, but it's not really necessary for you to **relax when you go into trance** . . . because it certainly isn't universal. There was a psychologist at Stanford, Jack Hilgard, who did an experiment some years ago to debunk the idea that relaxation is hypnosis, and he had people ride exercycles and go into trance . . . and experience various trance phenomena . . . like amnesia, anesthesia, hand and arm levitation. Even though they were showing all the signs of physiological arousal from riding the exercycle, while the induction was going on. So you can have muscle tension and you can pay attention to that tension and you can be **comfortable** knowing that you can **go into trance** with that tension being there . . . that it isn't something you need to work on to let go of . . . or to work on to relax . . . that your trance could be involved with any muscle tension that you have or could be involved with a combination of tension and relaxation . . . and that's your particular trance. That although trance is usually typified by a sense of slowing down the heart rate, the breathing, again, it's not universal and it would be a good thing to know that sometimes your heart rate may speed up and sometimes your blood pressure may elevate, sometimes you may be so focused on whether you are going into trance or not that your attention is just . . . all caught up in that and that you find that you haven't relaxed, haven't slowed down, haven't found that sense inside of **stillness** . . . of **peace** . . . of **going into trance**. And how will you know when you are in a trance, will it be when your perceptions start to change? Your eyes may be open and a change in your vision . . .

you may develop tunnel vision . . . little auras . . . some other alteration in your vision, if your eyes are closed you may experience
some other change in your visual perception . . . maybe colors . . .
maybe something else altogether . . . maybe a change in the muscles in your eyes . . . maybe a change in your sense of where you
are . . . right now . . . you may be sure that you're not **going into
a trance** consciously . . . and you may be concerned consciously that you won't **go into a trance** . . . just let that concern be there
. . . and let yourself just draw on the background of learnings and
don't trust yourself to go into trance too soon too quickly because
you can in your own way have the sense to really determine if this
is a trustworthy situation, one in which you want to go into a
trance . . . one in which you are willing to go into a trance . . .
and figuring out what you are willing to experience . . . so remember again, to validate yourself for however you are **responding**,
because your response is your response . . . and that you consciously may be thinking that you are having some response and
you may only be aware at the unconscious level of other responses
that you are having . . . for example you may not have noticed
any alterations in the muscles, you may not have noticed any alterations in your sense of attachment to the hands and the arms. The
hands and the arms could become detached in your experience,
could in their own way, develop a trance or mind of their own
. . . earlier you saw someone have an experience of that hand
movement, that arm movement . . . I remember Jay Haley talking
about going to a workshop with Milton Erickson, and Erickson
asked for a volunteer and Haley . . . was surprised to find that his
leg was automatically twitching and almost pulling him out of the
chair . . . and the person just in front of him stood up just about
as he was to stand up or he would have come up for a demonstration. So consciously he wouldn't have thought that he wanted to
volunteer but there was something compelling about the invitation
. . . and obviously his body wanted to volunteer. His unconscious
mind wanted to. So how will you know when you are in that
trance? Will it be some kind of alteration like that in your muscular
experience? As you saw earlier, a sense of the alteration of the
hands and the arms, a sense of dissociation . . . from the hands
and the arms . . . it might be that you start to feel little twitches in

the muscles in your upper arm. It might be that you feel your heart pounding and that becomes central to your awareness and then as you go along, that heart rate could slow down — automatically . . . might be you feel **changes** in your forearm or your wrist and consciously you might be noticing some conflict about that and resisting it and that's okay, you can let that resistance be there. Unconsciously, you may find yourself already **starting to respond,** and that response would just on its own . . . because the unconscious could use that muscle tension . . . and turn it into movement if that is what it wants to do. For me it feels as if there is a force pushing underneath my palm . . . pushing the hand and arm **up** . . . a little at a time . . . and your conscious mind really doesn't know which hand **lifts** first, it may be that they **lift** together . . . maybe that . . . it doesn't **lift** all the way to your face or they don't **lift** all the way to your face . . . so you can experience that in whatever way is appropriate for you. And when I first started doing trance, I don't really know how I developed the habit . . . but somehow I started doing trance with my hands in my pockets and I could tell that I was deeply in trance when I couldn't feel my hands any more and I had a pretty good idea that the other person was in a trance as well at that point . . . so if your unconscious wants to . . . one of those hands could start to . . . on its own . . . in its own way **lift up** off the thigh, the arm could **lift** off the thigh . . . or both of the arms could **lift up** together or alone . . . and you could just follow that **movement** as it does . . . or what might happen instead or in addition . . . is one or both of those hands might go numb . . . or you could lose time or gain time. . . . I was working with a man who had phobias, he was a therapist . . . he was quite ashamed that he had phobias, that if his clients knew they wouldn't come to see him. He was ashamed of those and felt really inadequate. I told him I thought it was a generic therapist problem that whenever we had problems we begin to doubt ourselves. That we are entitled to problems just like everybody else. And one time he went into trance he had a double hand levitation, both hands **up** in the air, and I happened to mention, because I knew he had a good sense of humor, the idea of remembering the humor of your favorite joke without the intellectual content and then I told him a joke that I had heard recently. It was a woman who had a fear of needles, phobia of needles went to see her doctor, and she said, "Doctor I have a fear of needles, do you think acupuncture would help?" It was a joke that maybe could use a chuckle or two, but immediately he started laughing hysterically, disturbing the other clients in the other offices. I told him he shouldn't laugh so hard because otherwise I'd put all my clients in trances and tell them silly jokes, and he shouldn't reinforce me in that way. But he just kept laughing harder and harder and he laughed so much, that tears started to flow from his eyes, and I told him it reminded me of a Joni Mitchell song: "one minute she's so happy then she's crying on someone's knee, you know laughing and crying it's the same release," and he started to cry at the same time and he was laughing and then he started to cry profoundly and he was still laughing. "It felt so strange," he told me later . . . "to be laughing and crying at the same time." To have his hands up in the air but to be fully with himself at the same time. To be tense and relaxed at the same time. To be here and there at the same time . . . to be in trance and out of trance at the same time and it was a very profound and integrated experience for him to both be helping people's problems, be having problems himself and to be able to integrate those rather than have them be two separate worlds. When he got over his phobias, he said that he felt normal. I didn't like the word normal. I told him I didn't have any aspirations for him to be normal or for me to normal. He finally explained to me that he really meant adequate. I told him I was glad he felt adequate — that that's the way I had always seen him. As adequate and okay — even when he didn't see himself that way. It's interesting to know that you can direct your experience, and I would like to give you an opportunity to direct your experience wherever you would like to do, and I would like to give one of you an interesting opportunity, when I touch your knee, to have you come out of trance from the neck up and to stay in trance from the neck down, and I'll ask you a question or two and you can have an opportunity to say whatever it is you would like to say about your experience . . .

Wayne, you can open your eyes and come out from the neck up and tell me what you're experiencing now and what you've been experiencing.

WAYNE: My hands are numb and there was a time I wanted to cry but didn't . . .

BILL: Anything else?

WAYNE: No.

BILL: Okay, you can close your eyes and go all the way back into your trance. And if you need to, if you want to, you can have the numbness transfer to anywhere you might need it, to your knee or anyplace else, to eliminate all the unnecessary discomfort and still give you enough sensation to be able to . . . know to take care of yourself and to take care with yourself so that the healing can continue . . . even in an accelerated fashion. So you can feel more comfortable as you are healing and still attend to whatever you need to attend to . . . and now you may not be sure that you've really been in a trance . . . or you may be sure that you've been in a trance, but whatever your experience has been, make sure that you validate yourself for being where you are, for having responded the way you responded, give yourself permission to be exactly the way you are and to have had the experience that you've had, and when you are ready, at your own rate and your own pace . . . you can start to complete your experience of being in trance, and when you are ready, start to reorient your body the way it was when you first started sitting on that chair, let yourself experience what you experience, feel what you feel. There's nothing that you need to do particularly except just reorient to the present time and present place, to come back to your body sitting in the chair, to you and your body sitting in your chair. And when you are ready to come all the way out of trance, just reorient, open your eyes, and come all the way back. All right. Welcome back, gentlemen.

And what I'd like to ask from you in the peanut gallery is questions or comments, and for each of you [participants in the demonstration] to say a few things about your experience. The point of having three people in a demonstration is to show you similar kind of words produce wholly different kind of experiences and responses. It shows you how to talk in a way that doesn't intrude upon one person's experience when they may not be doing what the other person is doing. It's a little more of a challenge and uses a few Ronald Reagan words. Sometimes I was talking to one person and sometimes to all three of them.

AUDIENCE: What presuggestion did you make that all three of those guys have the same kind of shoes on. (*Laughter*) It's weird.

BILL: It was the soul induction I did earlier. Careful seating and selection.

AUDIENCE: Were you able to regulate their breathing patterns just by your speech?

BILL: Not particularly, I just went back and forth and after a while they sort of came a little to a middle ground, but they never were totally aligned. I just go to one person for a while and meet and match that person, and then another person for a while, and pretty soon they come a little more to the middle because my voice is sort of the pace after a while, but not always.

AUDIENCE: So that's kind of like a group trance?

BILL: Not kind of like, it *is* a group trance.

AUDIENCE: But not necessarily a common presenting problem.

BILL: They really didn't have a presenting problem. I knew Wayne had been through an operation and was healing, and that's really about the only thing that I knew one would want to work on. I put something about that in there in the end for Wayne, but I wasn't really working on that.

AUDIENCE: Well I guess my question is under what situation would I want to do a group trance?

BILL: Well, I suppose if they did have similar presenting problems that might be a good thing. If you were doing a group and wanted to do some trance with them in that particular setting. Or if you wanted to do a demonstration in a workshop.

AUDIENCE: Or maybe doing family therapy.

BILL: Doing family therapy, that's a possibility. If you have more than one person in your office and wanted to do trance with them, a couple whatever. That's good. What else? How about from you three?

WAYNE: I was surprised. I didn't think anything was happening, and surprised when I realized that my hand had moved. I thought maybe just one of them could do that and then the other did, too. The other surprise was that my nose started dripping.

BILL: That was the earlier suggestion you did and you got it now. We put a time release capsule on it.

WAYNE: A time delay, you said something about I might see colors, and I didn't see any, and then later I saw purple.

BILL: Are you a slow learner but trainable, is that it? Okay, that was interesting.

FRED: One of the things that happened at first just after we got into it was like I could see a tunnel. It was more like light, and it would narrow and focus, focus and get small, and go away and then start again. I had that some. And when you asked us to wake up from the neck up, it was amazing how dead I felt from the neck down. Not dead like I couldn't feel it, but it felt hot and numb and strange. I was also, I think, not ever unaware that there was an audience and I felt a little self-conscious of that and real aware of that.

BILL: Okay. Robert, do you want to say anything about your experience?

ROBERT: I think I felt like I always felt.

BILL: Not sure you were in a trance. Any other experiences within that experience?

ROBERT: No.

BILL: Okay. Other comments or questions on this?

WAYNE: I also have some of that question of "was I really in a trance," but I figure if I wasn't then that . . .

BILL: You don't usually do this (lifting up a hand) during one of your conversations?

AUDIENCE: Do you remember laughing out loud?

WAYNE: Oh yeah. I liked the joke about the lady who was scared of needles. What do you do with someone who seems to be uptight and holding on into a trance . . .

BILL: I keep giving them permission and finding out how they respond. Now the question is of the people that you saw up here, what did you see that looked like trance? Levitation—that was pretty obvious sign, again for Fred and for us. We say, well, not sure you are in trance, but that's a pretty good external sign. That's why hand levitation, arm levitation is a pretty nice sign, because it does look different from the usual way of moving.

AUDIENCE: What did you think when that happened?

FRED: I thought, holy shit, what's happening? (*Laughter*)

WAYNE: I didn't respond to it. Now, I thought, well thank God something's gonna happen here.

BILL: Good. What else did you see that looked like trance?

AUDIENCE: I thought I saw his finger move on his right hand, twitch a bit.

BILL: Yes, I thought he might do a hand levitation, I wasn't real attached to it, but I thought he might.

AUDIENCE: His hand was trembling at first, but then his other hand was about to go up.

WAYNE: I noticed that, too, but it seemed like this one wanted to go up.

BILL: The hand has a mind of its own, I guess.

AUDIENCE: Lack of facial movement . . .

BILL: Okay.

AUDIENCE: Robert, for a while there I thought that you were going to, that your breathing would remain the same but it changed, you kind of stopped chewing something, and I don't know whether that was intentional or not.

ROBERT: Yes, I realized I might have been distracting myself by doing that, so I stopped.

AUDIENCE: Your breathing got a lot more regular.

BILL: Less movement as you went on. Okay, what else?

ROBERT: Early on, my feet wanted to shift, and I didn't know if that was all right to do that or not, and you said to take care of yourself and I said, well it feels better, so I'm gonna shift 'em.

BILL: That's all right. Okay, what else? What made it seem as though they were in trance or not, what signs did you see?

ROBERT: I started to twitch with the hands and just completely stopped.

BILL: Yes, we saw the fluttering of the eyelids for a while, and then they got real still. All right, what else? So who would you say went into trance the quickest?

AUDIENCE: Fred.

BILL: You think so? I would have said Wayne. Wayne just got real immobile very, very rapidly, then Fred, and I wasn't ever sure whether Robert was in. At times I thought, "Yeah, he's getting into it," and then at other times I couldn't tell.

AUDIENCE: Have you found that with the hand levitations that it's more likely that in levitation they start out like this (with hands apart) as opposed to like this (hands clasped)?

BILL: A little more likely, but not 100% correlated. That's why I usually say to people, "Uncross your arms and uncross your legs." But I'm not real attached to it. Sometimes it's much more profound for people when their hands are together to have hand levitation because they think they are never going to move like this, and all of a sudden they are moving and coming apart. It's very, very profound for them. To have that conscious thought, "I don't think anything is going to happen here," or "I'm interested to find out what sort of thing will happen," and then to have something happen is very, very convincing.

AUDIENCE: Why were you unsure with Robert?

BILL: Because I saw some indicators that he was starting to go into trance, but I didn't see a lot. The breathing changed, he got more immobile. The eye fixation was happening pretty well. Then I saw some signs of moving around, shifting, the breathing wasn't always consistent, the facial muscles flattened out a bit but not as much as I usually see them in a trance.

AUDIENCE: The first exercise that we did, when I was watching Robert it seemed like he'd start to go and then there'd be some involuntary movement, and when we first did our exercise, I wasn't willing to go with that so I started to defocus, and my eyes would start to see, and then I'd start to bring myself back, and that seemed like that sort of in and out sort of thing.

BILL: Yes, and I had that sense, too. All I would say to do with that is a little more inclusion of that to make sure he knows that's okay and supported and so it's not like "Oh boy, are you resistant!" or "You're not willing to let go," or whatever. So it doesn't become an accusation, it doesn't become a failure, but it becomes, "Okay, you are learning whether you can do this and trust yourself in this situation and how you can do it." But I saw some of that same sort of stuff, and what I'd be doing if I were just working with him alone is doing a lot of communicating about and supporting of that.

AUDIENCE: Is it possible to say at the end of the trance that maybe he didn't go as deep as he wanted to and the next time he could go deeper?

BILL: Yes, absolutely. I'd link it to the next time, and I'd say he *could* in the future. Or that he was starting to get a little experience with it, which, and this is my absolute belief about it, he was starting to get a little experience with trance *and* he didn't go into a trance. He sort of put his little toe in a few times and that was about it.

AUDIENCE: And also that is the kind of thing I'd have, particularly with clients who are used to the traditional, as I was before coming here, caught going into the scary feelings of "I don't know."

BILL: Right. Or the opposite way, trying too hard, trying to make it happen. I want it to happen, so much that I'm gonna try to make it happen. Either direction—"I'm scared and I don't want to let go, and it's too tough," or "I really want this to happen, and I'm going to try too hard." Either one is antithetical to trance, so you have to find some way to include those and have them move towards trance.

Great, okay, good. Thank you for being up here and taking the risk to come up. I appreciate it.

Now it is time for you to practice eliciting trance phenomena— typically, the ways we elicit hand levitation. I need you to find the handout (3.2) entitled *Methods for Evocation in Solution-Oriented Hypnosis*. This fits exactly with what we want to do in this approach. We don't want to program people from the outside saying you *have* to respond like this, but give them a bunch of invitations

Handout 3.2

METHODS FOR EVOCATION IN SOLUTION-ORIENTED HYPNOSIS

Anecdotes; Stories; Analogies; Common, Everyday Processes, Experiences, or Objects

universal
specific to the person's background
    they've told you about them
    you've gathered indirectly or have guessed
imagery—usually given in a one-step removed manner
    specific; general/vague; different sensory modalities
situations/activities

Presuppositions; Expectations

rate
variations
before/after/during
awareness
multiple choice alternatives

Interspersal

emphasizing certain words or phrases nonverbally
puns

Direct Permissive Suggestions

possibility words and phrases

and a smorgasbord of possibilities for response. Then we notice which possibilities they respond to and amplify those by saying, in effect, "That's right, those hands can lift on their own." Once Fred started to show me that response I gave him a lot of amplification for that and support for that. Meeting him where he was and amplifying new responses in the direction I was suggesting. Once he starts to show me a response, I'll ride on it and start to link one response to another.

When I saw Wayne respond as well I thought, "Great! I think that Wayne is ready to do a body dissociation because he responded so well. He's been very immobile. That immobility suggests a good trance to me." My guess is he was having some feelings of numbness or dissociation or lack of awareness of where his body was, because he wasn't orienting to it proprioceptively. I thought he'd probably be able to develop a really good body dissociation. I though I'd give him the opportunity and thought it would be a nice thing, given that he's recovering from surgery on his leg, for him to experience that sense of dissociation, having his body work on its own. It had all sorts of implications. Once I saw that response I thought, "Great," ride on that.

In solution-oriented hypnosis, there are a bunch of ways to evoke experience rather than to add it from the outside. Using anecdotes, stories, common, everyday processes or objects, either universal ones (we talked about those before with the eating popcorn kind of thing and having your hand hit bottom, for dissociation), or specific to the person's background—either that they have told you about or that you know about indirectly or that you have gathered or guessed about.

David and I talked over lunch, so I knew that he played the flute. If I'm working with David I can talk about how your fingers can work automatically without you thinking about them when you are playing music. I know that if he was good enough to play in a band that he probably has had that experience of fingers operating automatically when he played the flute. He joked over lunch, "I used to not have much money and now I've got these boats and cars," now I know that he sails, so I'll start to talk about sailing or driving out on a lake or whatever. I've gathered some things about his life indirectly or directly from what he has said. So one thing or another that I know about a person I can use. (*To a participant in the front row*) I know that you juggle. I can talk about the little pieces of experience that go into learning and doing this thing called juggling. At first it was little muscle movements. While I'm talking about that, that can evoke hand levitation for you because you have done juggling, as your hands move now in response. Thank you, hand, for showing that response, that was nice. Use things that you have observed about them or they've told you about them or that you can infer about them.

Analogies. Use common, everyday experiences or observations.

Like the analogy of doing hand levitation when you say, "Imagine that a helium balloon is tied onto your wrist or fingers." Now in solution-oriented approaches, that's much too direct because if they don't visualize the helium balloon, they may think, "Oh no, I've failed." So what we usually do to make it less threatening is use one-step-removed analogies. For example, "Some people imagine a helium balloon tied onto their wrist or fingers."

We've already talked about **presupposition** and **expectation** in terms of inducing a trance and with hand levitation and arm levitation: "I wonder which hand will lift up first." You'll hear Erickson do a few of these in this next taped example.

Interspersal, again, involves emphasizing certain words. Did you notice while I was working with Dennis how much I interspersed words? I said, "Now your unconscious mind can come **up** with certain things and you can **face** certain difficulties, and it's nice to know your unconscious can help you **move** towards goals." I was emphasizing certain words: **up, move, face, hand, arm**. Some of those words were emphasized as nonverbal emphases, interspersed suggestions. Sometimes they were puns, sometimes direct words.

Direct permissive suggestion: "That hand can lift up, the arm can lift up, the hand can feel numb, you can wake up from the neck up and stay in trance from the neck down." General permissive empowering suggestions. All right? We'll see and hear a couple of examples of Erickson doing this in the taped examples I'll play for you now.

Videotape Example #2: Milton Erickson—
Hand/Arm Levitation (1958)

The first example is an excerpt from a tape made in 1958. Erickson was at Stanford, and his work was being studied and they were filming him. He's just been introduced to this woman, and one of the first things he says to her as she sits down is, "Are you forgetting about the lights?" because they have these big, bright lights to do the filming. And what's that a suggestion for? Negative hallucination. He just asks it, sort of presumes it. And she says, "Oh no, should I?" He says, "Oh no, but you can, you know." Then he starts in with his invitation to experience hand/arm levitation.

ERICKSON: And I'm going to take hold of your hand in a moment or so. Now, as you watch your hands, they're resting there. And do you know about the feelings you have when you are feeding a baby and you want the baby to open its mouth, and you open yours instead of the baby? And did you ever put on the brakes when you were in the backseat of a car?

RUTH: Yes.

ERICKSON: Well, I would like that same kind of automatic movement. Now look at my hands. You see very, very slowly, without it being a voluntary thing, my right hand can lift and it can lower. And the left hand can lift and lower. Now what I'd like to have you understand is this: that you have a conscious mind, and you know that and I know that, and you have an unconscious mind or a subconscious mind. And you know what I mean by that, do you not? Now you could lift your right hand or your left hand consciously, but your unconscious mind can lift one or the other of your hands.

He gives her an example of common, everyday experiences of automatic muscle movement. You want to feed a baby. You open your mouth when you want the baby to open its mouth.

ERICKSON: And I'd like to have you look at your hands, and I'm going to ask you a question. And you do not have to know the answer to that question consciously, and you'll have to wait and see what the answer is.

Here he's inviting her to focus her attention.

ERICKSON: I'm going to ask you: Which hand is your unconscious mind going to lift up first? The right hand or the left?

"Which hand is your unconscious mind going to lift up first, the right or the left?" Good use of presupposition. He's presumed that a hand is going to lift up, possibly both hands (because he asks which hand is going to lift up *first*). He also presumes that the unconscious mind will lift the hand.

ERICKSON: And you really don't know. But your unconscious knows. That's right. And it's beginning to lift one of your hands. Lifting, lifting, lifting, lifting up. And now watch it. That's right. Watch it lifting, lifting, lifting. Up it comes. Lifting higher. And watch it. Soon you'll notice it. And keep watching your hand and watching it. And if you wish, you can close your eyes and just feel your hand lifting higher and higher. That's right. Lifting still more. That's right. Elbow will start bending and the hand will come up. That's right. Lifting, lifting. And now close your eyes and just feel it lifting, and it's lifting higher and higher. And I'm going to take hold of this hand. And it's lifting, lifting, lifting, lifting. That's right. And the other hand is lifting, lifting up. That's right.

Now I kind of like this segment because I've had enough experience to understand that Erickson didn't get a good response. There is this attribution of omnipotence with him but this shows, as you can see, he's saying, "Lifting, lifting," but it's not lifting. But Erickson's mastery wasn't that he always got every response he tried to elicit, but that if he wasn't getting it one way, he'd go for it another way—he was very persistent, and he was very creative. So, he decides, okay, she's very compliant, but she's not doing levitation, so he just induces catalepsy. He lifts both hands up, induces catalepsy and then he does this wonderful thing where he suggests that one can go down and one can go up. He links those two together—so if she's going to express resistance by not lifting up her hand, he's given her the chance to express that resistance by having it go down, but she's now being responsive by resisting. She's responsive in a way that is resistantly responsive. So it's a clever move, I think, and a nice way to do it.

ERICKSON: Now I mentioned before that the hand could lift and it could go down. And now I wonder if you know which hand is going to go down first? One or the other is going to go down. And down it comes. That's right, that's right. Down it comes, down it comes, and coming down still more. Still more. Down it comes, down it comes.

"So, which hand is going to go down first?" He uses the same presupposition he used before only this time it's about going down. One starts to move, and he says, "That's right." He's reinforcing and amplifying that response.

ERICKSON: And as it comes down, I want you to go deeper and deeper into the trance. I'd like to have you enjoy going deeper and deeper. And when your hand reaches your lap, you'll take a deep breath and go even deeper into the trance, because you're beginning to learn how now. That's right, coming to rest there. That's right. Now take a deep breath and go way deep asleep.

Now, he gets another response and links that with going deeper into trance: "As the hand goes down, I want you to go deeper and deeper into the trance." Then, he links enjoyment to going deeper into trance. Then, he links taking a deep breath and going deeper into trance.

ERICKSON: And now let it seem to you as if many minutes had passed. And I'd like you slowly to arouse and look at me and talk to me. And slowly rouse up now, slowly rouse up, rouse up now. And open your eyes. That's right. And you're beginning to learn to go into a trance. Do you realize that?
RUTH: I think so.
ERICKSON: You think so. And how does your hand feel?
RUTH: Um—a little heavy.

"Do you realize you are beginning to go into a trance?" Presupposition, implication, behaviorally, linguistically, both in that one-minute span there. You notice she could hardly find her voice there, that changed voice quality I talked about there.

ERICKSON: A little heavy; and can you see your hand plainly?

RUTH: The one in my lap? Yes.

ERICKSON: And this one?

RUTH: Yes.

Again a suggestion for negative hallucination, "Can you see your hand plainly?" Why would you ask that? It is implied that she can't or won't be able to sometime in the future.

ERICKSON: Now watch that hand as it gets closer and closer to your face. That's right. That's right.

He never told her to move that hand, he just said, "Watch it as it gets closer and closer to the face." It starts to move and he reinforces that response: "That's right." She starts to smile.

ERICKSON: And I would like to have you pay full attention to the sensations of the movement of your arm, the bending of your elbow, and the way that hand is getting closer and closer to your face.

So, he just wants her to pay attention to the sensations, the movement of the elbow, implying it's going to bend, now all he wants her to do now is attend to it.

ERICKSON: And very shortly it is going to touch your face, but it's not going to touch your face until you are ready to take a deep breath and to close your eyes and go way deep, sound asleep.

Here he has used linking by giving a contingent suggestion.

ERICKSON: That's right, almost ready, almost ready. That's right, that's right. And it's moving, moving. That's right. And you're waiting for it to touch your face and getting ready to take that deep breath. Getting ready to go way deep, sound asleep in a deep trance. Almost touching now, that's right, almost touching now. And yet it isn't going to touch until you are ready to take that deep breath and your eyes will close. That's right. Getting closer and closer and closer. That's it, elbow bending more, fingers move up to touch your chin. That's right, that's it. Almost there, almost there. And now your head starts bending forward. That's right. And you'll take a deep breath and go way deep asleep. That's right.

Handout 3.3

EVOKING AMNESIA

Analogies/Stories/Common everyday processes or objects
—Vault/safe/wall/room/box/sealed envelope
—Sand flowing through fingers

Anecdotes/Common everyday experiences
—Name or fact on the tip of the tongue
—Looking at a picture and not remembering being there for it
—Hearing family members tell stories about things you've done but don't remember doing

Presupposition/Expectation
"How much will your unconscious mind choose to have you forget?"
"When will you discover that you have forgotten something?"

Interspersal
"And I don't want *you* to *forget* to take care of yourself in any way you need while in trance."

Direct permissive suggestion
"You can't remember to forget all that you need to forget."
"You can leave behind in trance the things that are for trance and bring out of trance the things for your conscious mind to recall."

Amplification of Response
"That's right. And you can forget other things besides your hand."

Here he's attributing, linking, describing, and reinforcing her responses.

Handout 3.4

EVOKING HAND/ARM LEVITATION

Analogies/Common everyday processes or objects/Images
—Helium balloon
—Ball of energy pushing underneath the palm
—Block/tackle

Anecdotes/Common everyday experiences
—Putting on the brakes from the backseat or passenger's side
—Opening your mouth to get a baby to open his/hers
—Trying to move the bowling ball after it leaves your hand
—Parent reaching out to hold child when stopping quickly in a
  car

Presupposition/Expectation
"How quickly will your unconscious mind lift that hand and arm?"
"Which hand will your unconscious mind lift first?"

Interspersal
"Your unconscious mind can *come up* with something that can let you know it is working for you."
"You can let your unconscious give you a *hand* in *moving* towards your goals."

Direct permissive suggestion
"Your hand and arm can lift up to your face automatically."
"It can lift even more. That's right."

Amplification of response
"That's right. Lifting a little more now."
"And those little movements can lead to bigger movements."

The preceding handout details analogies and experiences that can be used to evoke hand and arm levitation.

So you just saw Erickson do this hand and arm levitation thing and I'm going to help you learn to do something similar with some exercises today and tomorrow. I want to make sure that you know how to conceptualize this process. So I've given you two handouts that summarize the process of evoking amnesia (forgetting) and hand and arm levitation.

I've detailed some of the common analogies and experiences that you can tell the person in trance in order to evoke experiences of amnesia or hand levitation. These examples are followed by examples of using presupposition, interspersal and general permissive suggestions. Once you start to get a reported or observed response I've given some phrases that you can use to amplify and extend the response you've gotten.

You can use these handouts to help you understand and follow the next exercise and then tomorrow you may want to use them as cheat sheets. But the main thing I want you to get from them is a way of thinking and methods for evocation. Remember, your job is to invite people in permissive and indirect ways to experience things that are automatic and either deepen their absorption in trance or lead to resolving their presenting concerns.

Okay, good. I have an exercise, and this exercise we'll do in a different way. You're all going to do this exercise tomorrow, but right now what I'd like to do is have two people come up here and have me be your coach. You'll do it in a fishbowl fashion and I'll be your alter ego, giving you some ideas on how to do it. I have my eye on a couple of people. *You*, Sharon, because you are such a trance junkie. Have you ever done hand levitation in trance before? Oh, you say you've never been in trance before? Well, I saw you go into one earlier, okay. I'd really like you to do the induction if you are willing, Priscilla. Okay, good.

What I'm going to do is be Priscilla's alter ego. She's going to start out and maybe think, "I don't know what to say," but I'm just going to tell you what to say if you get stuck and you will just repeat my words as if I didn't say them. Speak on the exhale and go for inviting hand and arm levitation. Again, don't get attached to it happening. Me and Milton Erickson are back here doing it, and you're going to speak to Sharon and say, "How will it happen, when will it happen, in what way? Will the finger move first, will the thumb move first?" and all that stuff. Then, if you can think of it, think of everyday analogies that you or Sharon might have had, automatic hand or arm movements. Especially involving the hand and arm, doodling, or raising your hand in class.

I have a few hints for you. Use empowering suggestions: "The hand might lift up, the hand can lift up." You might also emphasize or intersperse suggestions for hand levitation, like "up and lift." "I went to England and instead of calling them elevators, they call them **lifts**, so what you've got to realize is that each culture has it's own idiosyncratic language." You might talk about someone trying to **muscle** in on your territory or whatever it may be. You can emphasize those words, **muscle, lift,** and **arm.** I used one, "Dennis, it can be pretty dis**arm**ing the first time you have hand levitation," to suggest dissociation from the arm and also to mark out the word "arm." So, you are going to be using any or all of that stuff. Your job is to make as many mistakes as you can and to feel awkward and stuck, and I'll just feed you lines. But, initially, just start out with the trance induction, and if you only get a few words out, great, or a couple of sentences, that's fine, and I'll jump in as soon as I have something to say.

Exercise #3: Fishbowl Induction and Levitation

PRISCILLA: Sharon, as we are doing this just breathe any way you want to and I'll catch the rhythm. So . . . and a little bit earlier we talked about whether or not it was more comfortable for you to open your eyes or close them, which would you rather do for this?

SHARON: Close my eyes.

PRISCILLA: Okay. So you just breathe normally . . .

BILL: Rather than "breathing normally," "you **can**," so it doesn't sound like a command, so if she's not breathing normally, she'll think she's supposed to. Okay.

PRISCILLA: And if you feel like smiling or frowning or whatever, that's good for you to do that just whatever . . .

BILL: I wouldn't say, "that's good," I wouldn't emphasize the things that I don't particularly want more of. But she can smile if she wants, and that's okay, but if her hand moves, I'd say, "That's right," or "That's good," or "That's fine." But if she smiles, it may be a bit of a distraction for her. I just *allow* that, rather than reinforce it. Okay.

(Bill's comments are in parentheses.)

PRISCILLA: And somewhere in the past, I'm sure that you have had an experience where you had to lift your arm to do something like lifting groceries out of the car, especially when they get down in the trunk of the car and you really have to reach for them and lift them up. And I'm wondering if possibly we might get some hand lifting this afternoon. (as you go into a trance . . .) As you go into a trance, (even if you're not consciously sure what a trance is yet) even if you're not consciously sure what a trance is yet, possibly your arm will lift. (I want to presuppose that the arm will lift, so I don't want to say, "possibly your arm will lift." I could say, "Your hand and your arm can lift up automatically, and I really don't know whether it will right away or as we go along in trance." Now, as I say that and as you were talking, the fingers and thumb started to move, and I would start to attend to that and amplify it, "Now it may be that you notice that your thumb is moving.") It may be that you notice that your finger and thumb is moving, and if you do, I'm wondering which (hand is most likely to lift first . . .) hand is most likely to lift first (which hand does she think is most likely?) which hand is most likely to move first. Your unconscious mind knows, and I'm wondering which one it will choose. (Or will it be both?) Or will it be both? (and move at the same time) And they may move at the same time.

(Now you want to time your suggestions for lifting to her inhalation. If you watch her upper arm as she breathes, it tends to move up, and her hands tend to move, so we better time the suggestions for lifting.) So when your unconscious decides which one will be the one to move first, or both . . . ("It can lift," time that to that breathing, because she's right on the verge of having that lift off her thigh, that's right.) That's good, it's lifting, lifting. (But will it lift all the way to the face?) (*Sharon laughs.*) Sorry. (It's kind of weird to be watching and listening to this whole process, isn't it? That's why I chose you, Sharon, 'cause I knew you could listen to this, be amused at the same time and still have it happen, so just get back into the kind of trance that's appropriate for you, that's right.) Movement is beginning. When some people go into trance, they giggle. (Some people do hand levitation by going into trance. I would assume she is already going into trance or is in trance a bit, and now I'd just be working on hand levitation. "And continue in that process and be interested and amused by it." And now once you've got the response, be leading all the way up or to another response, speculating how far it will lift, if it will lift all the way to her face, whether she'll notice it or whether she'll lose track of it while it's lifting, whether it will go in a straight line, all those possibilities. But now I'd have my visualization about it touching her face and lifting up more. So I'll be quiet for a minute, and you can say more.) And I'm wondering as your arm is lifting, where it's going, is it going to lift straight up or is it going to lift out and up, is it going to lift directly to your face, lifting, up, whether it will lift to your nose, or whether it will lift up to your cheek and I'm wondering if you think that's pretty silly, now, but it's lifting and when? When it will lift up all the way to your face, lifting, I'm wondering if there is some doubt, while it's still lifting? (That's nice and inclusive.) And I'm also wondering as it lifts, how long it will take, but that's okay, as it lifts closer, lifting closer, lifting higher? My mind is wondering whether or not you can bend your head to meet it.

(Now I'm going to give you another tangent to go on. She's learning something, going into trance and that's nice and having hand levitation which is new for her, but you might as well link the hand lifting then to a personal goal that she has, link it to her personal motivations. Now you know Sharon better than I, maybe you have talked to her a little, but what I know right now is she is wearing a crystal. So she probably has some new age kind of ideas and is probably into healing, like many therapists are. So why not link the lifting of the hand to some personal healing she'd like to have happen? Something personal, getting in touch with herself spiritually, because then it will be more motivation for that hand to lift up to her face, so the motivation comes from inside of her rather than the outside. So if you can link it to that, that would be nice.) As that hand is lifting, Sharon, I'm wondering whether or not it would be something that you would want to have happen when your hand touches your face, when it lifts up to your face, that you could have some type of confidence, achievement, whatever you choose, happen for you. (Now, I would link it to this workshop, a sense that you've been really integrating the learnings and that you've developed more and more confidence about your ability to use trance in a way that is both right for you personally and professionally. That's another thing we know about her. She came to a hypnosis workshop, she probably wants to learn this.) Your hand is lifting more rapidly now, and when it touches your face you'll have a feeling of confidence and competence. (You're on pretty good ground to say "you **will**" but if she doesn't, then we are in deep trouble. Because she's already showing so much response in this, I think it's likely that she would, but it's a little too directive.) Lifting up, lifting more rapidly, and when it touches your face, you can realize any goals you set for yourself. (or any particular goal) Lifting and I'm wonder as your hand is lifting, lifting to your face, the realization, the confidence, that those goals you have set for yourself can be achieved, lifting . . . almost there. (That's right . . .) That's good, almost there . . . (so close you can almost taste it) You are very close, you're almost there. (And I'd like to invite you, Sharon, after it touches your face, take just about 30 seconds of clock time, and you can come out of trance.) Very close. (With that hand up there, or you can have that hand go all the way back down.) You can have that hand where it is or you can choose to let it come back down. And take a few seconds to reorient yourself to this time and place. (That's great, good, terrific.)

SHARON: That's the weirdest damn thing I ever did.

Oh, I bet we could find some contenders, but one of the weirdest, we'll buy that. We could ask your friends that are here. (*Laughter*) No, no, they're not going to tell. Well, good, good job, good job, terrific, all right. You went for it, and you did it, that's great. Why choose Sharon? She's a trance junkie like me. I knew she would be very responsive. As I'm teaching, I watch you all and watch how you respond, and I get a sense that some people are pretty responsive. I had the sense with Sharon that it wouldn't be too intrusive for her for me to be talking while she went into trance.

I have a sense you people are getting this stuff. I'm happy with the day and your responses.

When we get back here in the morning, we are going to get to the punch line: Why would you ever do trance; what's trance good for? We are also going to be taking up the topic of what the unconscious mind is in this approach. And if the unconscious is so smart, as Erickson implied, why do we have symptoms? We are going to be taking that up tomorrow, having you do more practice. The practice tomorrow, though, will not just be namby-pamby, wishy-washy stuff like, "You can do anything you want and go anywhere you want in trance," but will be about getting specific responses, like hand levitation, like time distortion, like age regression, things that you specifically go for. We'll have another answer tomorrow for the question of why to use trance phenomena in treatment. We'll give you a clear model for treatment, what you do once the person gets into trance. So you have gone for it today, you have learned a lot on the conscious and unconscious level, I'm sure. And I suppose you all know what dreams are for, so I suggest you use your dreams in various ways for your benefit tonight to integrate the learnings, to expand the learnings or just to help you get a good night sleep so you can be fresh to learn even more tomorrow.

FOUR

Why Use Trance?

THIS MORNING WE GET TO the punch line. Why would you ever use trance? What is hypnosis good for? You've gotten along fine in your clinical practice without using hypnosis so far, so why do you need it now?

To answer these questions, we have to start with the question: What is the unconscious? In the Ericksonian approach, when we use the word "unconscious," we mean something different from the Freudian view of repressed urges and primal urges that the ego or the superego have to deal with. Erickson used the concept in several different ways. One of those views is a little like the Freudian preconscious, a repository for those things you don't keep in your conscious mind, but could recall if you wanted. Another Ericksonian definition of the unconscious is that it is your deeper, wiser self. A third definition is that the unconscious is your jukebox of learnings, that is, your jukebox of memories. When you press the right button it stimulates a certain brain operation and you remember certain things. It's like a jukebox of information that you have stored that you don't keep in your conscious mind and perhaps couldn't deliberately recall. So it's not even preconscious. In this third definition, the unconscious consists of sensory memories that you have from your life.

The third definition is more relevant to what we are talking about this morning. The third view refers to all the stuff you have on automatic pilot. Erickson used to say, "Trust your unconscious." And you'll hear Ericksonians saying, "Your unconscious is creative and smart, it's a wise part of yourself, much wiser than the conscious part of yourself, which is limited because of the limiting beliefs that you hold consciously."

I have a friend, Joe Barber, from Los Angeles. You'll hear some of his stuff on a taped example in a little while. He can be a very critical kind of guy, and he doesn't like the Ericksonian movement a lot with all this "guru-fixation" of Erickson and the purple pajamas that people wear. He knows I'm a little irreverent as well. He and I went out to lunch at one of the Erickson conferences and he said, "You know, these Ericksonians are driving me crazy running around saying, 'Trust your unconscious, your unconscious is smart and creative.' Don't they know the unconscious is dumb, dumb, dumb?!" he exclaimed. It challenged me pretty well because I must admit *I* was thinking the unconscious is smart and creative, having been influenced a lot by Erickson. So, I thought it's a good thing to think about, since it's good to challenge those fixed and rigid beliefs that one has. Over the years I sorted it out for myself, and this is what I've come to. My view is that the unconscious is smart about the things it's smart about, it's dumb about the things it's dumb about and that there are some things that the unconscious is smart about that it is dumb to be smart about. Now this is not a confusion technique—this is clarity. So let me make it clear for you.

Let's start with the idea that your unconscious is smart about the things it is smart about. That means if you know how to play tennis, and you go on out and practice tennis, and you've really gotten good at it and played and practiced and taken lessons and you played a whole lot, you're a really good tennis player. Then you should go out on the tennis court, and when you play tennis you should trust your unconscious. Your unconscious is smart about playing tennis and you should get out of the way, because if you are trying to play tennis consciously or think about it consciously, you'll be a much worse tennis player. If you know how to touch type, you should trust your unconscious to touch type, don't look at the keys, don't think about it. If you think about how you do it, it'll go a lot slower and harder. One of the definitions of the unconscious, it does things automatically. When you know how to drive a car you do it automatically, you don't have to think about how to put on the brakes or put in the clutch, once you learn it and your unconscious gets smart about it, you don't have to think about it.

I could do this lecture and play guitar and play a fairly complicated thing on the guitar *while* I was doing a lecture, because I've got both doing the lecture and playing guitar on automatic pilot. Therefore, my unconscious is smart about playing the guitar. If I got a banjo, I couldn't stand up and play. I couldn't stand up here and just let it flow through and let the *muse* inspire because the *muse* would sound pretty terrible through me at this particular point. So my unconscious is dumb about playing banjo, smart about playing guitar. My unconscious is dumb about playing tennis, so I shouldn't go out and trust my unconscious because I wouldn't do very well. I should play very deliberately and try to learn it and think about it a lot and practice a lot, mess around and make mistakes and that would be how my unconscious mind would get smart. I would have to do it a lot to get smart about it. My unconscious mind is dumb about the things it's dumb about. I don't know how to touch type, I'm not a good touch typist, so just hitting any keys that seem right to me wouldn't work.

Now to the last category I mentioned — sometimes the unconscious mind is smart about things it's dumb to be smart about. What I mean by that is back to the naturalistic approach of Erickson. Sometimes we get naturally smart about things it's dumb to be smart about in certain contexts.

Say I was sexually abused or physically abused many, many times when I was younger. And how I learned to deal with that as a coping mechanism was to dissociate my body from the rest of my experience. Like Wayne did yesterday. Only he dissociated his body in a directed, guided way. When you do it spontaneously throughout your life because you've been abused you get really good, really smart at dissociating automatically. It's a really good thing for you to do to survive sexual abuse, physical abuse, it seems that people do it a lot spontaneously, and it's a great survival skill. Unfortunately, then what happens is you grow up, you get out of that context of abuse and go into another context. Perhaps you get married, or get into a relationship and your partner starts to approach you sexually and you dissociate. You're not there anymore. It's not a threatening situation, because your partner has never abused you, but your unconscious is so smart about dissociating that you do it automatically. You do it unconsciously. Your unconscious is smart about something it's dumb to be smart about in that setting.

Or say for years it's been really a good idea to notice pain that you have because it served a signal value for you. Now you've got some chronic pain that doesn't serve any signal value for you at all, it's just chronic arthritis pain or you are dying of cancer. Now it's not so useful and smart to notice pain but you've had years and years of practice of noticing pain. So your unconscious is smart about something it's dumb to be smart about in that context.

That leads us to the questions: Why would you ever use trance? What's it good for and not good for? Somebody asked me this question a while ago. When would you use hypnosis or when not, or do you just use it all the time? No, sometimes my clients have no idea that I use trance unless they find a brochure while in the waiting room and they ask, "You do hypnosis?" They may not have a clue, as it was never appropriate to use it with them. Some only know that I use trance, they don't know I do anything else. Someone years ago said, "When do you decide to use trance or not use trance?" My response was that I know in the first session with the client whether I'm going to use trance or not. My rule of thumb is to divide the world of symptoms or problems into what I call **voluntary** and **involuntary complaints**. That guides my decision about whether or not to use trance.

Voluntary/Deliberate Activity Complaints — Contraindicated	**Involuntary/Automatic Complaints** — Indicated
Actions Interactions Deliberate (nonautomatic) thoughts	Somatic/physiological difficulties unresponsive to medical interventions Experiential difficulties Obsessive/automatic thinking Affective difficulties Hallucinations/Flashbacks

Voluntary complaints are those that the person could produce upon request. If you asked them to show you their symptom, problem, or complaint, they could do it. **Involuntary complaints** are those that they couldn't show you upon request. Complaints aren't involuntary if people say they can't help it, because almost everybody in therapy is saying on one level or another, "I can't help it— help me." I'm just saying, could they do this problem deliberately if you requested it? So if someone came in and said, "I smoke, help me stop smoking," I could say, "Show me your problem." They could pull out a cigarette, put it in their mouth, light it up, inhale, flick the ashes off the cigarette and show me what that problem looks like. Now if they said, "Every time I walk into a shopping mall, I break out in a rash," I could ask them to show me their rash. And they'd say, "I can't, I don't know how to show it to you. Come to the shopping mall and I'll show it to you." That's involuntary.

If they say, "I yell at my kids," and I say, "Okay, give me an example, show me what you do." They could do the yelling: "You little blah blah, go to your room." They could show you what they did. If they did bulimia, they could show you how they did it. You might not want them to show you, but I don't usually ask them to show me in the office. If they said, "I've got migraine headaches, can you help me?" I could say, "Okay, do a migraine headache so I can see how your family reacts when you have a migraine." They would reply, "I can't do that, come to my house when I have one and maybe you could see one then, but I can't really do one for you." Migraine headaches, rashes, various things like that are what I call involuntary complaints. Yelling at your kids, smoking, eating in certain ways, those are voluntary complaints. I'm not talking about what they *claim* about it, I'm just asking myself, is this something they could reproduce upon request or not? I think hypnosis is great for involuntary things and not so good for voluntary complaints.

Why? This gets back to what the unconscious mind is. Because I think hypnosis is really good at changing automatic internal experiences. Your unconscious is really smart about those things you consciously don't know how to change. For example, if I said, "Okay, tell me how it could be. What could you do instead of yelling at your kids?" They say, "Well, I could go in the other room and cool off." They could do something deliberately to change that. But if you said, "Tell me what you could do instead of having a migraine headache," they would say, "I don't know. I've taken medications, tried to relax to reduce the stress in my life. I don't know what I could do." They don't know how they do migraine headaches, and they don't know how to not do migraine headaches. That is, if they did something deliberate, it probably wouldn't interfere with their migraine headaches or rashes. If they did something deliberate, it would probably interfere with their smoking or yelling at their kids, or beating their spouse or whatever. Typically, voluntary complaints are actions and typically involuntary complaints are internal experiences.

AUDIENCE: Where would you put depression?

It depends on how they do it. Now you can construe depression as a voluntary complaint primarily, or you might put some elements of it over in involuntary land. Usually, depression is a combination of actions that people do, cognitions that they have and feelings that they have. I usually put depression in voluntary land and don't usually use hypnosis with it. You might construe it a different way and if you did, you might use hypnosis with it. Some things are probably somewhat a combination of voluntary and involuntary, but you can ask yourself, what are the main features of it? That's what I'm suggesting.

Think of something like school phobia. Sometimes when I've investigated it, it is actually school avoidance. If it is school avoidance, it is mostly voluntary, the person's just not going to school. It's called school phobia because that's the common name for it, but it really is just not going to school. And then sometimes there's a fear part of school phobia that is a realistic fear, like somebody is going to beat them up in school, and they are afraid of that. And that's not really phobia, it's a fear and there may be some actions they could do to change what they fear. Perhaps they could interact with the kids differently or maybe go to a different school. Now there may be a phobia part of it, and that is they have the palpitating heart, of they have sweaty palms or they are shaking or nervous, and that stuff you might be able to do something about with hypnosis. But, ultimately, even if you change the phobia part, you are still going to have to get the child to walk into school. Even if you change the desire to have a cigarette, you are still going to have to have the person change the habit of smoking cigarettes, which is an action. You can divide it into two parts: the desire to smoke a cigarette, the relaxation they get from smoking a cigarette, those internal experiences are the involuntary parts, and the voluntary part is the smoking behavior.

I base my treatment on my assessment of whether the main features of the complaint are voluntary or involuntary. For me, the main feature is the activity of smoking. In flashbacks from sexual abuse the main feature is involuntary and experiential. Hypnosis is great for involuntary stuff and not so great for voluntary stuff. Now you might be thinking, "Wait a minute, those hypnotists who advertise in telephone books and the paper almost always advertise for smoking and weight control." Well, that's good marketing because those things make a fair amount of money, but the actual research seems to indicate that about 25% of people with those complaints do pretty well with these approaches and the rest of the people don't over a two-year follow-up. It doesn't seem to me a coincidence that about 25% of people are highly suggestible and highly hypnotizable. Maybe they are not the same group. I don't know if they have ever been compared, but some people would do well no matter what approach you use, and if it's a suggestion or placebo approach they'll do pretty well. But I don't think hypnosis is very useful for treating voluntary action complaints.

I think hypnosis is profoundly useful and a new set of skills for therapists who have previously only had the skills to treat voluntary complaints. When I first started doing hypnosis, somebody came to me with warts as a presenting complaint. Now as a therapist, rarely did anybody come to me with warts as a presenting complaint. It was smart of them not to come to me for that, because I didn't have even a clue about how to treat warts. The only way I could have thought to treat them was if I convinced myself and the client that warts come from stress. Then maybe I could reduce your stress to eliminate the warts, because I, as a therapist, know how to reduce stress. But in hypnosis I knew exactly how to work with warts.

So typically over in involuntary land I'd put physiological things, somatic things, and I would put some kinds of thinking, that kind of intrusive automatic thinking we call obsessive thinking. I'd put voluntary, deliberate kinds of thinking in the voluntary category. If I ask you to imagine yourself being assertive and you imagine it, that's deliberate thinking. But there is some kind of thinking that is obsessive thinking, intrusive thinking that seems to think itself. It's as if you don't think it. For example, did I turn the stove off back home, did I lock my door, or obsessive thinking about a former relationship. That kind of stuff. Hallucinations are perceptions that intrude upon your experience involuntarily. Over in voluntary land, it's actions and interactions and certain deliberate kinds of thinking.

Why do I think hypnosis is good for involuntary things? Because as we said yesterday with trance phenomena, it lets you put your hand on the control knob of **experience**. It gives you a way to change experience. When you see these stage hypnotists who have people up on stage in hypnosis and get them to eat an onion as if it's an apple, you are witnessing people's ability, through hypnosis, to change what seems like an involuntary experience. The hypnotists say to the subjects on stage, "This is really a nice, juicy apple. Here, take a bite of it," and they do and really enjoy it, and everybody in the audience is amazed. For some reason, hypnosis gives us an ability to alter our internal experience. So that an apple taste can come from our memory, that experience can come even while chewing an onion. Or so that you can, during an operation, control the bleeding. Usually that's a fairly involuntary skill for most people. If I just said, "During your operation on your knee, Wayne, control the bleeding," you'd say, "Okay, I'll try, but I don't know if I'll be able to, I'll be knocked out." But, I could say to Wayne's unconscious mind, "While you are under that general anesthetic, it's really important for you to bleed just enough to clean the wound and not worry the surgeon and then stop bleeding," and we could probably have an effect one way or another.

Kay Thompson, who studied with Erickson for a while, shows

a tape of her getting a nose operation in which she doesn't have any anesthetic and stops the bleeding. It was pretty gross to watch but very impressive. She just deliberately arranged for spontaneous changes in her physiological functioning and in her experience. She somehow achieved a change in the bleeding and a change in the perception of sensation.

My father-in-law went through a bone marrow extract using self-hypnosis. He had no anesthetic, I guess they don't give them for that anyway, and he was perfectly comfortable and it freaked the doctors and nurses out because they couldn't tell when they got to the core of the marrow because they usually have people squirming all around and have to hold them down. But here he was just perfectly comfortable, and they didn't understand because he didn't tell them he was using self-hypnosis. He heard all this hub-bub behind him, and he asked what the problem was and they said, "Usually with people, it's very, very painful when we hit the spot, and that's how we know we got there." He immediately cancelled out the idea of pain they were suggesting to him and substituted an idea that he would feel some different sensation to let him know that they had hit the spot. So he said, "Oh, I didn't know you needed to know that—I'll tell you when it feels different." Somehow he was able to change what, for most of us, would have been a pretty involuntary experience of pain. For some reason, hypnosis gives us an ability to get our hand on the control knob of experience. I don't know why exactly, although lots of people in the hypnosis field will give you theories, but I don't think anybody exactly knows why yet. All we know is that it seems to be able to do that for certain people for certain things.

What do you do once you get in trance, what's the point? To be able to give them access to their natural abilities to alter their experience. Again, we in the solution-oriented hypnosis field believe they already have natural abilities. And what kind of alteration of experience do we want? We want to re-evoke skills and abilities that they have had, sometime in their lives. Like those of you who wear glasses, you've learned to negatively hallucinate your glasses, to drop your glasses out of your experience. That's a nice skill. Although you probably never thought of it as a skill. It can be considered a skill, though, which we can evoke in trance and then amplify, so that you would maybe go through an operation without noticing the sensations of the operation. As Kay Thompson did. That's negative hallucination.

If you've learned naturally in your life to dissociate because of abuse, why not be able to use that skill to be able to see the trauma, instead of having it flashback and have to feel the traumatic experience happening all over again. Why not use that ability to dissociate but channel it and guide it in a certain direction, so now they can see it as if it's on a television screen or movie screen and use that natural ability and keep their bodies feeling comfortable while they watch the trauma when they review it. What we are trying to do is, instead of having the old stuff happen, which is problematic, we are going to use whatever natural abilities and skills they have, amplify and direct those skills for their benefit. Remember the man I mentioned yesterday when doing the trance, the therapist who had phobias? After he had experienced the double hand levitation and laughing and crying in trance, he noticed that when he would go into one of his previously phobic situations, he would feel this sense of absurd amusement and feel dissociated from the fear. He would notice the anxiety but not get so hooked up in it. Where he used to feel anxious about being anxious, as many people do, now he would step back and observe that he was getting slightly anxious and he would think it absurd and be totally amused by it. Gradually, the phobias went away, in part because he wasn't getting involved in them anymore.

So what are we about when we do this kind of trance treatment? Evoking abilities, previous solutions, and patterns of experience. If you have taken lots of hot baths and relaxed a lot, you have a pattern of experience or previous ability to relax your muscles. If you've ever gotten a massage, you might have a memory of relaxing your muscles. Using trance, you can edit and reorganize your experience. You can split some things. Like the phobias this one guy had. He had a phobia of going into large open places, like shopping malls or big supermarkets. He had another one of if he were driving on an interstate in the middle lane, he would feel freaked out like he was going to faint. If he saw anything medical, he would also have these panic attacks and feel as if he were going to faint.

What we did was split off fears from those situations and linked in humor and absurdity. So we split and link. You want to make new associations and break old associations. There's nothing about walking into a supermarket that is inherently anxiety provoking, but he made that linkage in his experience. Looking at medical things on television would for him be linked with a certain anxiety or panic, but it doesn't need to be. Just as looking at spiders or snakes doesn't need to be anxiety provoking, but some people have themselves wired up like that. We want to help them split certain parts of their experience, make distinctions they hadn't made before. You'll see this in some of the work with sexual abuse that I'll show later and with some of the other examples. You want to link in some new associations, new linkages, alter people's experiences in some way. For example, you might have them experience a tingling instead of a pain. In working with women who are going to give birth, instead of focusing on pain, you could focus on the anticipation of what this child is going to be like. What color eyes will the child have? How much hair will the child have? You could look forward to the personality the child will have. There are all sorts of things you could focus your attention on. Instead of focusing your attention on painful sensations after your operation you could focus on aspects of the experience that are comfortable.

So, how do you do it? What are the techniques? It is a lot of what we talked about yesterday in terms of methods of evocation in solution-oriented hypnosis. You tell anecdotes, stories and you use common, everyday processes or objects that correlate with what you are trying to evoke. You use interspersal, you use metaphor, puns, presupposition, empty words, and general permissive suggestions. The point is what we are going for is not just telling people new ideas and reprogramming them, but **evoking experience**. We want them to have an experience. Hypnosis is really good for helping people have experiences. I could say to Wayne, "Look, you can dissociate your body, did you know that?" And he might say, "Yes, I guess so, it sounds credible to me, it sounds possible." But when he has an experience of it, it's much more powerful than when I just tell him about it. And hypnosis is really good at creating experience. I could say to Wayne, "Dissociate your body right now," and he might say, "I don't know how to do that, I mean I had it yesterday, and maybe I could do it again, but I don't think so." But if I went through the rigmarole of doing trance with him and said, "Now wake up from the neck up and keep your body in trance," he could do it, probably would do it, especially since he had done it before. Somehow, in some way, instead of having somebody talk to you and just tell you good ideas or reprogram you, or send you back into your childhood and get repressed memories, what we want to do in solution-oriented hypnosis is to have you experience something that will give you access to new possibilities.

My goal is not to go for an explanation of your problem, not to reprogram you with what I think will be good positive beliefs for you, but to give you an experience of something that's a resource for you, something that could change the situation for you. I think that's the difference between therapy that really has an impact on people and therapy that is just a bunch of clever, good ideas. The good ideas may just go in one ear and out the other. But it makes an impact when it really gets into their experience, and makes a difference for them.

So, that's the point and the methods. I've tried to give you a clear simple model for when you do trance, why you would do trance, how you would do trance, and what you do when the person is in trance. Next, I'll have you practice some more and have you generate these kinds of interventions in therapy, how to approach a particular case. We'll have you practice some more in terms of the skills and do some group brainstorming on how to think about certain cases, given a particular model called the Class of Problems/Class of Solutions model. Before that, any questions?

AUDIENCE: On some of the voluntary behaviors like smoking, can't you approach them with hypnosis by linking them up with involuntary behaviors that can control their behavior, like imaging the taste of an onion when you smoke a cigarette?

One can, and it has been done and done successfully. It wouldn't be my preferred approach to it. Because I don't think it works too well. The literature and my experience indicates that usually it doesn't work very well for stuff like smoking and weight control. The person that it works for, it works for 100%, but overall it's not a widely effective approach.

AUDIENCE: Is it still the 25%?

Yes, people have used aversive techniques, projecting people into the future to anticipate being a non-smoker, and it does work a bit, so I don't want to say it never works for voluntary complaints, because hypnosis has been used for just about everything. From cancer to bed-wetting to misbehavior. I just think it's not wildly effective for voluntary complaints. Although it does work on occasion. On occasion, I violate my rules of thumb and just use it with a voluntary complaint because it makes sense in this case or I have a good intuition it's going to work or because nothing else has worked and I might as well try it, what the heck. But it wouldn't be my treatment of choice. But your question indicates that you've got the point of what I was saying hypnosis is good for; the point being you would access some involuntary experience and link it to the voluntary complaint, which might change their experience of it, their behavior.

AUDIENCE: Can you see any connection between Ericksonian conscious/unconscious with the gestalt foreground/background thing and would that have any value in explaining hypnosis to patients?

Sure, I think that you could make some connection between those two. It would be a fairly simple connection. "Foreground" is what's in the conscious mind and "background" is what is in the unconscious mind. I don't know about explaining it to people, but using that particular model with somebody might have value. My sense about how to do therapy and what to do in therapy is much more oriented towards solutions than explanations and much more oriented towards evoking abilities and skills, rather than spoiling interventions—having the cigarettes make you nauseous or taste like onions. What I'm interested in is evoking abilities and skills that are much more pleasant abilities and skills and linking them to things that are pleasant associations. If that works for that particular person, I'd go for it.

AUDIENCE: How about tics?

I would typically call that complaint involuntary. Here's how I think about it. How would I do a tic if I were a body? Not *why* I would do it, not what function it serves, not the explanation about it, but what's the actual process of the doing of it? Now, usually it's an involuntary process, the way people report it, and it's a muscle spasm. How would I do the opposite of muscle spasm, then, what resource might I use for that? One resource one might use for that is muscle relaxation. Here in the person's experience, go and *evoke*, don't *teach* the muscle relaxation, because in the solution-oriented approach we'd assume they would have a skill called muscle relaxation. So where could I go searching for it? One way is I could ask them, "Have you ever taken a hot bath and not really been thinking about relaxing when you got in the bath, and when you got out of the bath you realized how relaxed your muscles were?" That would be one way to evoke it, to say in novelistic detail how relaxing that experience may be. "Even when your mind was going a mile a minute and you were really tense, thinking-wise, your body, because you were in that heat, just couldn't support the muscle tension. Perhaps you had 100 plans for when you got out of the bath, but then you decided to just lay down for a while, relax a little more." You are going to evoke that experience for the person and then transfer it to the problem context. Think of the *doing* of it, evoke a resource that would be the opposite of what you could use for this and then transfer it to the place where it's needed.

Exercise #4: Evoking Hand and Arm Levitation

Yesterday you saw these courageous people come up and do this wonderful demonstration in which Priscilla hypnotized Sharon (p. 103). That's exactly the same exercise I want you to do now. What we'll be doing is having you practice so that you can get up to speed about being able to do the hypnotherapy parts. This time you are going to go for a precise experience, not just go for allowing the person to have whatever experience they want to have. You are going to try to elicit a specific response. Like Priscilla was trying to elicit a specific response with Sharon of having her hand lift up to her face. Use these techniques that we've been talking about. Speak on the exhale, evoke hand or arm levitation by using presupposition and implication, that is, "I don't know when the hand will lift up, how quickly it will lift up, which hand will lift up, etc." Never doubt that it's going to lift up, and once it starts lifting up, never doubt that it's going to lift to the face. Even though it may not lift up or lift all the way to the face, never doubt that in your speaking. Next, use anecdotes and analogies for hand and arm movement. Any reference to automatic movement will work, like feeding a baby and having your mouth open, putting on the brakes when you are sitting in the passenger side or backseat of the car. But especially hand and arm movements. So come up with a few of those. Let's brainstorm a few. I'll give you one to start with, but you'd have to be fairly old to know this one, I think. You'd have to be old enough to have kids before seat belts were common. When you put on the brakes in the car and you reach out automatically for the kid in the seat next to you to restrain him. You may still do that even though they are now in seat belts.

AUDIENCE: You do it and there's no kid.

You reach for the kid and now there's no kid there, but you do it because you are so used to it. Like Erma Bombeck tells the story that she knew she had been with young kids too long when she was invited out to an important dinner with a bunch of business people and diplomats. She was in a fascinating conversation with a guy next to her, some diplomat from someplace important, and they were having a great time and the guy all of sudden looked at her with a look of horror on his face. She looked down and realized that she was cutting up his meat. (*Laughter*) So you could tell that story about automatic hand or arm movements. All right? What other kinds of automatic hand or arm movements can you come up with, so to speak?

AUDIENCE: Brushing your teeth.

Great. Most people go unconscious while they brush their teeth.

AUDIENCE: Stretching.

Good. What else? I talked before about doodling, how about taking notes at a seminar?

AUDIENCE: If you are used to a beeper on the belt, and if somebody else's goes off in the room you reach for yours.

Right, you automatically reach for yours, that's good. Come up with a few examples that especially have to do with hands and arms and automatic movements. I'm talking about ones that happen automatically, like when somebody throws you a ball unexpectedly and/or examples that involve dissociated movements. We should include both categories. Use those anecdotes or analogies. Analogies would be the helium balloon tied to your hand. Sometimes I say, "For some people it feels as if there is a force pushing up underneath their palm, for some people it feels sort of like a block and a tackle, with a chain attached to their finger or wrist, pulling it up a little at a time."

I'll remind you again that when you use analogies, make them one-step-removed analogies. Not "Visualize a block and tackle pulling your hand up," but "Some people do . . . " or "One could . . . "; don't say, "*You* do this." That's too much pressure and much too directive. Use empowering permissive suggestions: "That hand can lift up automatically, it can lift up without you lifting it up, your unconscious mind can lift it up." Not *could* and not *might* and not *probably*, but it **can**. Possibility. Use interspersal— interspersing the suggestions by emphasizing them nonverbally, words like **move, lift, up, arm**, and **hand**: "Your unconscious can keep a lot of knowledge **hand**y for you and can **come up** with the right knowledge at the right time. It can help you **move** towards your goals and **face** things that you hadn't **faced** before." Okay? "And I really don't know if you think that **that hand can lift up** and maybe you are consciously sure that that **hand** won't **lift up**."

Again, I remind you to time your speaking with the person's exhalation. Now, I want you to do a quick experiment. Put your hands on your thighs. Do a couple of quick breaths, in and out and notice what happens to your hands and your arms when you breathe in. When you inhale the chest lifts up slightly and your hands lift up slightly. So if you tell the person, "Your hands are lifting up," when they are exhaling, it's not going to be congruent with their experience. You might as well wait for the inhale to make one of those lifting suggestions then. I want one talker this time and one listener. Take about 20 minutes. I'll be around coaching you, I'll be your alter ego if appropriate and may feed you lines.

(*The participants do the exercise.*)

Okay. Start to put your attention back into the big group. How many people experienced hand levitation for the first time in their lives? Let your hands raise slowly. All right. Questions, comments?

AUDIENCE: The difficulty I had was, again, concentrating, watching the breathing, looking for those signs.

Right, that was a fairly common thing. Here I was going around observing these wonderful responses. I could see that the listener's hand was starting to move, and I would say to the talker, "Great, you're getting it!" and they would look surprised, like, "What? I am?" Because I was really focused on the hands, not being distracted by having to think about what to say, I could notice some beginning signs. As soon as you see that response, reinforce it and amplify it.

AUDIENCE: One time I saw Robert's arm twitching and I got all excited, reinforcing it, but that was it.

That was it, just twitching a little. So you just go for it. And what I suggest with David is you just go with it and maybe after a long time of doing that, if you are still not seeing a very noticeable response, there are two things to do. The first is to go for very, very small micro-movements rather than go for this big, big thing of lifting all the way up. Just concentrate on eliciting slight movements of the thumb and the finger. The other thing is to say, "Okay, one of your hands can be glued to your thigh and can feel so heavy it won't come up." Then you put all the heaviness into one hand and maybe the other hand gets freed up to lift. Because perhaps hand levitation was a good idea, but not one that moved your listener greatly. He might prefer to stay still.

> AUDIENCE: I think having permission to go real slowly was good, he was using the clock and I could feel something moving, and I felt like I should move it but maybe I didn't have to do it that fast. Also, it was kind of like a split. I could feel movement and was thinking I want to do it this way. Also, I was consciously thinking about one hand and the other one goes up.

Did it surprise you that the other one went up then?

> AUDIENCE: Yes, because I was much more focused on the one.

> AUDIENCE: Could it be that some people just don't do hand levitation, like some people don't do windows. I could put them in a trance some other way maybe? That's not a major handicap?

No, they could be in the slow learners' class. I would say that for the most part, what you've got to do is go for it to the maximum *and* not be attached to it. When I'm inviting levitation, I have this sense of really going for with this person *and* I'm not attached. As soon as you get attached there is the possibility of failure. Go for it, and then if it doesn't happen, cut your (and their) losses and move on to something else. There are lots of ways into trance and lots of ways to get an involuntary muscle response besides hand levitation.

AUDIENCE: One thing I noticed was that yesterday I was deeper in trance at times. I would come back and hear Linda's voice and I know I didn't hear all she said, yesterday. Today, I heard everything. And I guess with me it was like a control thing. I started out thinking, I'm gonna make her feel bad, and then I thought, this is okay, I can open my eyes and I am more aware than I was yesterday.

Well, it speaks to a couple of things. One is there is this idea that only in deep trance do you do these trance phenomena. That's not necessarily so. Obviously not, given your experience. You were in a lighter trance than you were yesterday. The other thing, for some people, hand and arm levitation invitations will tap into some control issues and for them, and they'll be monitoring a lot more. Another aspect is that trance can be really interesting, and I suspect that for most of you, some part of you was analyzing and thinking, "I wonder if it's going to happen? No, I'd rather it be this hand or that hand." So one part of you is commenting on the process, observing it, thinking about it, deciding about it, and another part of you is having the experience. That's dissociation. One part is observing, commenting on it, while the hand is just lifting up, and you are in that experience, with that experience, having that experience. Okay? What else?

AUDIENCE: Getting back to the thing from yesterday, I realize that there was very much a sense of control there, and if I had Sharon in the office and she started giggling, I would have said, "Hey that's it, it's not working, let's get out of here." Because I was very, very uncomfortable with that.

Right, so sometimes what you have to have is a little persistence and a little faith in the process and not bail out so quickly, deciding that she can't do it or you can't do it. Just stick with it. Have a little faith. Somehow give the listener the sense that she's not a failure if she doesn't do it. It's not terrible if she doesn't do it. It's just something you were asking for. It's an invitation with a RSVP, rather than a demand. Don't make it a demand.

AUDIENCE: How I experienced the process of being the one who does the trance induction is I go kind of blank. It's been real interesting to sort of observe myself because the kind of permission-giving phrases that you use a lot, I use a lot with clients in my work and never thought of it as hypnosis. But I'm not pulling them up quite so well when I'm right there in front of the other person.

So use your notes.

AUDIENCE: I was, I did, but I just wonder if other people are experiencing that kind of "What do I do now?"

Yes, a lot of heads are nodding. You are normal.

AUDIENCE: I'm used to trusting my intuition, where you just sort of go through stuff, that's what I usually do, but it's not pulling up so fast.

Exactly, because you don't know how to play tennis yet. And trance induction is like tennis. I mean how can I stand up here and teach? Where's my notes? How can I sit up here and do all these trance inductions? For me, those things are on automatic pilot. Now, you do therapy very intuitively, very automatically, but you didn't when you first did it. You were saying, "They've got clients they are putting in the same room with me, oh no, what am I supposed to say to them?" This will happen with hypnosis, it will come. But in order to get to that place you've got to do more practice, practice, practice.

AUDIENCE: It's interesting how much easier it was today than when I was the subject yesterday.

Well, she's obviously better than I am.

AUDIENCE: Maybe I was the one who was better.

It was probably a combo. Okay, another comment?

AUDIENCE: Say, for instance, that you had somebody and they were just twitching or something, but that's all. Would you take them all the way through the exercises and say, "That's okay, it's just an invitation, blah blah blah," or somehow in the middle of the exercise, say somehow like, "That's as far as you need to go, it looks like this is it . . . "?

Either one or both. I don't have a general rule about that. I'd say it depends on your intuition of where the person is. For an exercise like this I'd prefer that you go all the way through, partly because of what Priscilla and I were just discussing, that sometimes the skill is persistence. It's about not giving up. Sometimes you tell people to do something and it works really well, and then they come back the next session and say, "Well, it's not working anymore." And you ask, "What do you mean?" And they say, "Well, we're not doing the tasks you suggested we do." And you say, "What do you mean it doesn't work? It works fine when you do it, it doesn't work when you don't do it." It's the same thing, sometimes persistence is one of the skills of therapy and say, yeah, it probably won't work if you don't do it. You can't just sit around and talk about it, you are probably going to have to do some things outside the office to master the learnings from inside the office. If you persist a little, past the doubts and the fears, often that can be an empowering thing. Of course, it's not always empowering — at times it is like beating your head against a brick wall, and that's not so good. I would just use my intuition. For an exercise like this, I did want you to persist.

AUDIENCE: Did Milton Erickson always talk to people that weird, or did he just talk to them like that when inducing a trance?

He seemed to talk to most everybody that way most of the time. If the mailman rang the doorbell, he tended to talk to him like that. He was doing trance and therapy most of the time 'cause he was just a wild and trancey kinda guy.

AUDIENCE: I was sitting here wondering, what might happen if instead of talking to people in therapy as I ordinarily do, I started to talk to them the way I have learned here. Like watching their breathing and. . . .

They'd go into trance, spontaneously without you doing anything else.

AUDIENCE: I'd have to figure out what I was going to do before they got there.

That's a whole different question: "Oh, oh, now they're in trance. What am I gonna do?" I think that's what Erickson did— that kind of conversational induction for the most part. Sometimes Erickson would do formal inductions in which he'd say, "We are doing a trance induction, uncross your arms and legs," and sometimes he'd do conversational and sometimes he would mix the two.

AUDIENCE: I wish I could start to talk without saying anything.

Well, I think you've got a little ability in that direction, Fred. I've had a few conversations with you. (*Laughter*) Sometimes it's like poetry and you just get a certain sense of the structure of it after a while. Then there's the technique level of it, where you just practice and practice until you get it.

FIVE

The Class of Problems/Class of Solutions Model

W HAT I WANT TO DO IS GIVE you a simple model for how you can generate interventions once the person goes into trance. Because the question is, once you get them into trance, what do you do? You've got their hands up in the air, and you say, "Great, I've got a response, what do I do now?"

I call this idea the Class of Problems/Class of Solutions model. I'll tell you how I came up with this. I moved from Arizona to Nebraska where I live now. I started a private practice soon after I moved to Nebraska. I didn't really know a lot of people in the area and, as those of you who ever started a private practice may know, I had a little time on my hands when I started. So I went back and reread everything that I had read about Erickson. I watched the videotapes, went back over the audiotapes, went back over my notes of my time with him and the notes I took from other people's workshops about Erickson. Sometimes Erickson would do an intervention or tell a story, and I'd wonder, "Where did he come up with that?" The person would come in, say, for bed-wetting and, all of a sudden, he would be telling them a story about playing baseball. And I'd think, "What does this have to do with bed-wetting?" He would do hand levitation as his treatment for bed-wetting. Or he would do hand levitation for impotence.

Handout 5.1

CLASS OF PROBLEMS/CLASS OF SOLUTIONS MODEL

Specific ---------------> Specific Intervention --------------> **TRANSFER**
Presenting   Analogy   **TO**
Problem   Anecdote   **PROBLEM**
                                Trance phenomenon   **CONTEXT**
                                         Task
                              Interpersonal move

```
   D                              E
   E                              V
   R                              O
   I                              K
   V                              E
   E
```

Class of Problems ----------------> Class of Solutions
                                    (Pattern of experience)
                                    (Resource/skill)

AUDIENCE: I can see the connection right there.

Well, you can see it, but the rest of the people can't yet, so we're gonna fill them in, Sharon. I couldn't see it at first. He would go from here to there, and I would wonder how he made that journey. He might make some specific intervention of eliciting one of those trance phenomenon we talked about, like levitation, anesthesia, time distortion. Or he would use an analogy or an anecdote or give a task assignment. He didn't seem to have any standard sort of intervention. He would use what you would call an interpersonal evocation. He would somehow evoke something in a person, get somebody mad at him or do something else that somehow would create some experience for them by interacting with them in some way. He would use one of these specific kinds of interventions, and I just couldn't get how he would leap from the problem to the intervention until I started to think about it in terms of this model: Class of Problems/Class of Solutions.

What occurred to me was that Erickson wasn't thinking in straightforward connections, he was thinking in terms of **descrip-**

tions, evocation, and analogy. From the specific presenting problem he would make a description of the doing of it, the activity
involved in generating the particular problem. For example, the
person might be doing bed-wetting. So what's the *doing* of it?
Remember that we're not speculating about *why* the person does
it, that's an explanation. We're talking about the doing of it. How
would you *do* bed-wetting? In my mind, there are two ways to do
bed-wetting. One is to have lack of automatic bladder muscle control. If you made it into the class of problems, a general category
that includes the specific problem of bed-wetting, you could say
"lack of automatic muscle control." The other way to do it is to
not have the signal of attending to it of waking up if your bladder
is too full. But you can do either one and be a good bed-wetter.

Okay, so the presenting problem is bed-wetting and the class of
problems is lack of muscle control. Then, the way I would think
about it, the way Erickson would think about it, is to immediately
think of a class of solutions, a set of skills or abilities that would
help the person. A pattern of experience or something in the person's background that one could evoke that would be the opposite
or the solution to lack of automatic muscle control. Obviously in
this case the class of solutions is automatic muscle control. So the
question is: In what places in the person's life might they have or
could they develop automatic muscle control? Sometimes Erickson
would find out or assume that they already had the automatic
muscle control built up. Sometimes he would give them experiences
so they would build up that resource or pattern of experience.

Okay, back to automatic muscle control. How could you evoke
that? Listen to some examples: One is a kid who wet the bed and
came to see Erickson. Erickson found out the kid played baseball
and his brother played football, and there was a bit of a rivalry
between the two. Erickson dismissed the parents, got them out of
the office, but didn't talk to the kid about bed-wetting at all. Erickson didn't even mention bed-wetting. He said, "I hear you play
baseball." The kid says, "Yeah, I play baseball." Erickson says, "I
hear your brother plays football." The kid says, "Football, yeah,
my brother plays football." Erickson says "Well, in my personal
opinion, football is a sport for gross, uncoordinated muscles." The
kid looks a bit more interested and says, "Yeah." Erickson says,

"Now baseball, that requires fine muscle coordination. Are you a good baseball player?" The kid says, "Yeah, I'm a good baseball player." Erickson says, "In baseball, the ball is hit to you and you open up your glove, you have to position your body right beneath the ball to get it. You do that automatically, you don't have to think about it, you open up your glove at the right time and the ball falls into your glove. Then you clamp down just at the right time to hold the ball in the glove and then, when it's time to transfer it to the other hand, you have to open up the glove just at the right time. Then you clamp down your other hand to catch it. When it's time to throw it home, if you let go too soon, it doesn't go where you want it to go. If you let go of it too late, it doesn't go where you want it to go. If you let go of it just at the right time, you can throw it home, where you want it to go. That's success in baseball. Now that takes fine muscle coordination."

Erickson asks the boy, "Have you ever done archery?" The kid says, "No, but I want a bow and arrow set for my birthday. I'd like my parents to get me one." Erickson says, "Well, it's interesting, because with archery, you notch the arrow in the bow, you look at the arrow, you look at the target, you look at the bow and arrow and the target, all the time you don't really realize that while you are aiming that there is this little round muscle in your eye that's closing down just at the right time, opening up just at the right time, to help your eye focus. Now I suppose you don't even know how you digest your food." Kid says, "No, I don't know." Erickson pulls out his anatomy and physiology books and shows the kid. "There's your intestines." The kid says," "All that's in me?" Erickson says, "Yeah, all that's in you. What's interesting is the food goes into your intestines, into your stomach, and there's a muscle at the bottom of your stomach that closes down and holds the food in there long enough for you to get the vitamins and minerals and nutrients out of it that you need. Then when it's time to get rid of the stuff that you don't need, that little round muscle at the bottom of your stomach gets rid of the stuff you don't need and then closes down again. It does that automatically. It moves the food all the way through all the little parts of your intestines. All those little muscles work automatically. If you tried to digest your food deliberately, you would eat your breakfast on Saturday and then spend your whole day trying to digest your food. You wouldn't be able to do anything else. Luckily your body handles that on its own."

Now he does a bunch of this kind of talk with the kid and, after a while, he sends the kid away, never having said anything about wetting the bed. And the kid stops wetting the bed. Now what's that about? It becomes obvious with this model. Erickson has construed it as lack of automatic muscle control, tells the kid a bunch of stories to evoke the experience of automatic muscle control and then sends him away. It's obvious why the kid's in his office, working on bed-wetting, so he never has to mention the connection. Sometimes you might make the connection a little more explicit. Okay, that's just one example, but you might think, "Everybody attributes all this wonderful wisdom to Erickson, but that's a big leap from just one example." But there's example after example of Erickson using this same class of solutions for bed-wetting and enuresis.

A kid comes into Erickson, a 12-year-old who is having trouble with his mother. The mother wants him to stop wetting the bed, and she really hassles him a lot. She makes him wash his own sheets, has punished him by telling the neighbors about his problem, has made him stand up in church and confess this in front of the congregation, etc. Sometimes she thinks the problem is genetic because the boy's father didn't stop wetting the bed until he was 17, and mother's brother didn't stop until he was 19, but sometimes she thinks the boy just wets the bed to frustrate her. So she goes back and forth between punishing him and feeling sorry for him. Father is disgusted with the kid because he's still wetting the bed, and father won't have anything to do with him. He's not doing well in school. Erickson asked what the problem was at school. His mother reports that his handwriting is really bad and that hurts his grades in all classes because nobody can read his handwriting so they never know whether he's giving the right answer or not.

So, his grades are pretty bad and he's also not very popular at school. Erickson again immediately talks to the kid alone and finds out a little about the situation. Next, he talks to the mother alone. Then he brings them back together and says, "I've got a plan for you. Here's the plan. Mother has told me the normal wake-up time for the family is 7:00 a.m. So mother, you are to set your alarm for 4:00 or 5:00 a.m. You go check your son's bed when the alarm rings. If the bed is dry, go back to sleep. If the bed is wet, get the kid up and have him go to the kitchen and practice copying pages out of his favorite book to practice his handwriting. While he is practicing, you are not to say a word to him about it, just supervise and make certain he does the writing. You can knit or do whatever while you are watching him. He is to continue this writing until the normal wake-up time of the family."

The kid was supposed to bring his handwriting practice in to Erickson every Saturday. Erickson had a special way of helping kids improve their handwriting and spelling. He would look at their pages and find all the stuff they did right. He'd say, "That is a great T, look at that T—it is right on the line, it looks really terrific. Now look at that CH, the way those two go together, that's really great." He wouldn't comment on anything else in the paper. And the next week the kid would bring another paper back and there would be more great Ts and great CHs and other good stuff and Erickson would again comment on the things that were right. Over time, the kid's handwriting improved a lot as he practiced and gradually he stopped wetting the bed. And you could say, well, it's an ordeal. Erickson made mother get up in the middle of the night, made the son get up in the middle of the night. That certainly makes it more of a pain in the butt to have the symptom than not to have it. That's one aspect of the intervention. And you could think, well, it's a family therapy intervention, it changes the interaction between family members. It is certainly that. But the aspect we want to focus on here is the class of solutions the intervention involved. The assignment had the effect of helping the boy develop automatic muscle control, and this time not by using analogies and anecdotes, but by evoking the same skill with a **task assignment**.

Now, what trance phenomena could you use to treat bedwetting? We have already talked about it: hand and arm levitation. Because what does it involve? Automatic muscle control. It's a great one for that.

One more example, this time using the last technique I have

listed as an evocation technique in your handout — the **interpersonal evocation**. An 11-year-old girl comes in to see Erickson for help with her enuresis. She has been cytoscoped and catheterized so many times (because she has had bladder infections for the past few years) that she has lost bladder control. The kids at school find out that if she runs after anybody, she leaks a little urine and wets her pants. So sometimes they grab her books and run away. She tries to run after them, but they know that she can't really chase them too far. So they tease her like that. Her sisters have found out that if they make her giggle, she'll wet her pants. So they make her giggle every once in a while. She also wets the bed occasionally. She is very proud and is greatly embarrassed about the enuresis.

She sees Erickson, and he says, "You already know what you need to know in order to stop wetting your bed and wetting your pants." She says, "No, I don't." And he says, "Yes, you do, you just don't know that you know it." She said, "You're right. I don't know that I know it." And he says, "But if you were sitting at home on the toilet urinating, and a strange man pops in the bathroom, what would you do?" She says, "I'd freeze." And he says, "That's right. You'd freeze and you'd stop urinating, and then you could start again, and then stop again, and then start again. And so all you have to do is go home and remember that strange man popping his head in the bathroom." Again, instead of telling her to go home and practice Kegel exercises, he has evoked for her an experience of that, of having muscle control, he evokes it in her interpersonally. He wants to evoke an experience of automatic muscle control. Once you've determined what resource you want, then you have to have them have an experience of it. You want them not just to know about it intellectually, and not just to practice it, but to really *have* the experience. That is what Erickson was doing on the tapes that you saw, evoking experiences, having the person *have* the experience and then master the skill. The next step is to transfer the skill to the problem context — to the context in which they need it.

Let me give you another example of it. Erickson used to say to people, "If you knew what I was thinking about you right now and all the things that I could think about you, you'd blush." Now that's a way to interpersonally evoke an experience of warmth, of blood flowing to the face. We could evoke that experience to help treat the problem of lack of sexual arousal. What's the "doing" of lack of sexual arousal? One way to "do" it is to have a lack of blood flow to the genitals. To treat it then, we can evoke an experience of increased blood flow to certain parts of the body. We could do that in various ways. We could tell stories about it. We could use trance phenomena and have the person's hand warm up automatically in trance. Or I could induce it interpersonally like that and evoke it, and then I could say, "And did you know your genitals could blush, too?" So that would be a way to transfer it to the problem context. You *evoke* it and you *transfer* it across. By telling stories and anecdotes, by using task assignments, by eliciting trance phenomena, and by interpersonal evocation.

Take, for example, the woman who came to see me for treatment of her warts. I mentioned her earlier. One of the things I learned from Erickson is that warts are very sensitive to the changes in blood flow. So I just copied an intervention I heard him do once for warts. I had her go home and soak her feet in the hottest water she could stand for 15 minutes and then the coldest water she could stand for 15 minutes every night when she got home from work. Now what's that about? When you do that, it changes your blood flow. And then during trance I worked on changing her blood flow.

I told her a story about when I lived in Casa Grande, Arizona, which is a community where they grow cotton. They had this interesting way of growing it. They have these little canals with water in them and then they have a berm or a dike to keep the water in the canals next to the field. They have these little sort of omega-shaped tubes that they put from the irrigation ditch into the field if they wanted to irrigate that part of the field. They plant cotton and when it starts to grow, they water it. But then little weeds start to appear so they pull the tubes out and they withdraw water from the field until the little weeds die back. And then they irrigate the field again and the cotton grows a little more, and when they withdraw it, the hot sun kills the weeds because they aren't sturdy enough. They'd just systematically withdraw the water from the weeds to kill them. It's the same with warts, I told her. "Your body can withdraw the blood support from those wart areas on your hands just enough to eliminate the warts, but not enough to damage the healthy skin. The woman had some warts on her face and feet as well. That's how I suggested transferring the skill of changes in blood flow to the problem context. I provided an analogy and gave her experiences of increased blood flow or decreased blood flow both in and out of trance and then transferred that skill to problem context.

I also told her the story about a time I was travelling over to Europe. It was September 6th, I remember. I was looking at my calendar, and I suddenly realized I had been scheduled to give a lecture at the medical school on September 3rd, and I had totally spaced it out. I was really embarrassed. I was blushing. I thought this is stupid, what good does it do me to blush? The person who had arranged the lecture wasn't there to see me blushing. I was travelling alone so I had no companion to see me blushing. But still I kept blushing. Finally, the blushing subsided, and I just vowed that as soon as I got to England I would call back and see if I could apologize to the person who had arranged the lecture and reschedule. A couple of minutes later, I was looking again through my calendar and again saw the date of September 3rd and started to blush again. Again, I thought, "What's the point of this?" But that didn't make any difference to my blushing, I just blushed. That story evoked blushing for her as I told it.

When I was a kid I used eat these little candies that were sort of lemon candies that were sour and tart. They would make me salivate when I would eat them. After a while all I would have to do was unwrap the candies and, in anticipation, I would salivate. Some of you experienced salivation as I told that. Now, if you were in trance, you'd be much more likely to get that experience, because we seem to be able to amplify your ability to respond experientially in trance. That story could be told to evoke an automatic physiological response.

For me, this model is a really simple one. What's the presenting problem? What's a description of the doing of it and the class of problems? What's a resource or pattern of experience the person could use to deal with that and how do you evoke it? Through hypnosis? Analogy or anecdotes, interpersonal evocation or through all of them? When you say "tic," I think, "Tic, what's the doing of tic?" Muscle spasms. What's the doing of *not* muscle spasms? Muscle relaxation. What's a way to evoke it? You could have the person feel really comfortable in your presence, and you might relax a little more. You could give them a task assignment of soaking in hot baths. You could have them get massages from their partners or friends. You could tell anecdotes about times when you or they were relaxed in the past, or analogies about how the muscles can just let go like all the strings on a piano being cut and all the tension goes out. You give them an instantaneous experience of muscle relaxation in trance. The difference between trance phenomena and teaching them relaxation is that in trance they could automatically relax, you don't have to take them through a whole long practice to experience it. You can *evoke* relaxation rather than *teaching* it to them.

Mostly the kinds of things that are classes of solution in hypnotic treatment roughly consist of the kinds of things that are trance phenomena. Why? Because the trance phenomena represent the kinds of things that are amenable to change with trance, but that are usually beyond our everyday control. With trance, we can change memory, perception, sensation, associations, and emotions. That's why I said earlier that the things that are most treatable by trance are the involuntary complaints or the involuntary aspects of primarily voluntary complaints.

So time distortion could be used to decrease the subjective length of the experience of pain or increase the subjective length of the experience of comfort. Negative hallucination could be used not to notice itching under a cast. Dissociation could be used to help a traumatized person remain comfortable while reviewing the details of their trauma. Age progression could be used to help a depressed person get a view of some positive possibilities for the future. We'll by applying this model and this kind of thinking to two particular problem areas after lunch: Treating the aftereffects of sexual abuse and doing pain control using solution-oriented hypnotic methods.

All right? Does that bring some clarity to the matter? Remember that clarity begins at home.

That's what I am hoping for you—to get clarity on what you do once the person gets into trance. That is what the morning has been about. Now this afternoon we are going to give you more examples, practice and demonstrations to help you integrate and apply what you've been learning.

Any comments or questions that came up over lunch? Perhaps "came up" is not a good choice of words. Did you think of something you wanted to ask or find out about, or did you want to say that this workshop was brilliant or anything like that before we move on? Yes?

> AUDIENCE: With the people that I work with, quadriplegics, is there anything other than facial flattening and relaxing that I can look at and observe that would give me some sort of indication the person was in trance?

Use whatever part of their body is responsive. If they had the ability to have changes in their facial muscles, you might develop a slight facial twitch here for a certain response so wherever they can get responses I would go for, if you are looking for observable ones. Otherwise you would probably have to go for unobservable ones that they could only report to you. And, I suppose another observable one that wouldn't involve muscles would have to do with the change in blood flow which you can probably see in certain parts of their body. Even with spinal cord injuries, you might be able to see changes in skin color and changes in blood flow. Sometimes you can watch the carotid artery. Yesterday, I was watching your heart beat, because your nametag was bouncing up and down in response to your heartbeat.

If you can pick something out that you can observe from the outside, you can make a suggestion and guide their association or invite them to do something and then see a response from it, that's what you are looking for. If you can't see any of that stuff, they could come out of the trance and say, "Oh, my hand went numb, or my face twitched or my face felt hot." It might be something you are not able to see but that they could report to you. And you don't have to see it—it's just nice to be able to check that you are getting some responsiveness. That's why hand levitation is so good because it's so obvious.

AUDIENCE: If you get a minimal response with hand levitation with people, I was wondering, would you try to frame that as a success in some way?

Absolutely: "I thought it was a success and maybe you thought it was a success too, maybe you never had it before. I would say your unconscious is obviously responding and might respond even more in the future. It might respond by lifting it all the way up to your face, or it might just respond in that particular way again, I don't really know." Yeah, I would frame it as definite responsive success. That would be good thing to do. (*To someone in the front row*) Did you have the sense that you were succeeding with the response that you showed, which was fairly minimal?

AUDIENCE: Oh, sure.

I thought it was a good response and a successful response.

SIX

Treating Survivors of Sexual Abuse

WHAT WE ARE ONTO NOW IS the solution-oriented treatment of survivors of sexual abuse. More and more these days, people are presenting this as a problem in therapy. I think more and more therapists are asking about it and just noticing it as part of the therapy. So the first distinction to make is, is the person *requesting* any help for this, or are you imposing it onto them because you've been to a workshop or read a book about this stuff? When I work on this issue, either people have asked me to work on it, or it seems obviously related to other work that we are doing. The basic question is "What does the person want to have happen in treatment, how will the person know that she's been successful in treatment, that it has worked?" Orient towards that. Make sure, of course, that the sexual abuse isn't current, that it is not still happening. You may be working on the aftereffects, *and* it's still happening. Obviously, this is much more likely with children, but it's possible with adults as well, that sexual abuse is still happening at this particular time.

Don't impose this idea that they have to go back and work through their traumatic memories. That's only one way to do it. Some people will do it a whole different way, and they can teach you and lead you in this process. Your job is to open up possibilities. Your job is to empower them to have experiences that will help them heal and move on.

Because most people that have been sexually abused are highly skilled at dissociating, you might as well use that skill. Again, this is a classic Ericksonian approach. We use the skills, resources, and abilities that people already have and consider what they are already doing as a potential resource. Even pathological mechanisms or coping mechanisms can be viewed and used as resources and skills. If a person has been repeatedly sexually abused, he or she is usually already good at splitting, dissociating their experience. So you can help them turn these splits from bad, self-destructive splits into helpful and healing splits. In psychotherapy, these people are usually viewed as damaged goods. We think they are messed up and don't have resources. Sometimes they have multiple problems and look as if they are really messed up. What we are oriented to in solution-oriented hypnosis, however, is determining what strengths and abilities they have. What resources do they have? Instead of finding out what function their problems serve or why they are messed up, we are looking for what capabilities they have and stimulating those resources and abilities to help them in the healing process.

What's important in any kind of treatment is to support and validate people the way they are. One must be careful not to support in a way that closes down possibilities by focusing so much on the pain that you forget the possibilities for them moving on. What I see in this work a lot is that we focus so much on how terrible it's been for the person and how painful it's been with the sexual abuse, that we wallow in that or hypnotically induce a focus on the pain of the past. The solution-oriented approach acknowledges where the person is, acknowledges what happened, and *then* opens up the possibilities for moving on. The orientation is towards solutions rather than back into the past. If the person goes back into the past, then you'd better go with them, but keep in mind, "Where is this leading ultimately? Where are you going? Where would you like to be when you know this is complete for you?" This approach is oriented towards the future, oriented towards solutions. The analogy I use is the sport of curling. Curling is this game that's played on ice. There is a stone or puck and it's like shuffleboard on ice. One team tries to push the stone to a certain target. The players sweep the ice smooth in front of the stone and channel it in a certain direction. I think it's much the same in therapy. I'm sweeping openings and a smooth pathway in front of the person. I'm acknowledging where they are, acknowledging the responses they are giving me, acknowledging their experience and, at the same time, opening up possibilities. I'm offering multiple-choice options. Then, based on their responses, on what they choose, I open up more possibilities. It's always multiple choice. Would you like to do this, this, or this?

I also consider the abuse to be in the past and the possibilities to be in the present and the future. So my message to them is, "You've been abused, that's your history." Sometimes they've been collapsing the past, present, and future together, so I start to make distinctions between the past, the present, and the future. The way I use language implies that the problem is in the past and the possibilities are in the present and in the future. You'll hear this on the videotape example. There are a few other things I want to say about this type of treatment, but right now I just want to show you the tape and we'll come back and speak about those other things.

Videotape Example #5: Bill O'Hanlon— Hypnotherapy for Sexual Abuse Aftereffects

This is a videotape of a woman who's been in a workshop on solution-oriented hypnosis for a few days. The last day is focused on the treatment of the aftereffects of sexual abuse. I've asked if someone in the audience has been sexually abused and has something unfinished about it. She's been reluctant to come up, even though she'd like some help with some situations she's been dealing with, because she remembers that she experienced sexual pleasure during the abuse, and she things, "Well, I'm not like all the other people that he's talking about because I think I sort of wanted it, I got some sexual pleasure out of it." Sometime during the day I made the distinction, "Sometimes people say that they had pleasure during their sexual abuse, that is, they felt experiences of physical pleasure. Then you can make a distinction between feeling physiological pleasure and wanting to be abused. Just because you felt physiological pleasure doesn't mean you wanted it or liked it. It's sort of like if you were slicing onions, and you started to cry, it wouldn't mean you were sad; you just had a physiological response to it." So she thought, "Oh yeah, that makes sense. Maybe I don't have to be so ashamed of this. Now I think I want to do that demonstration." So, she wrote me a note saying she wanted to do the demonstration. But, at that point, we didn't have too much time left, only about 30 minutes. I thought 30 minutes was a little limited, but as you'll see, the demonstration works out well.

For time purposes, I'll skip the part where I gather information, which I can summarize for you. What she tells me is that from the time she was born until she was 11 years old, she has no memories. Then from 11 to the present she has photographic, very vivid memories. She knew something was weird back in her childhood, she just didn't know what until recently. A few years before, while she was reading an article about somebody who had been sexually abused, it all came flooding back to her that she had been sexually abused. She thought at first that it might have been her father, because she had a flashback of her father passing by the barn window in which the abuse happened. But, after a while, she realized it was a 16-year-old cousin who used to take her to the barn and abuse her. She had the sense that she had somewhat willingly participated in the abuse to defy her mother, who was very controlling. She knew it was somewhat naughty and forbidden, and she had the sense her mother would disapprove. But she was upset and ashamed about it.

She had been doing self-hypnosis and had, over the course of several years, remembered most, if not all, of the abuse incidents. The memory blank had become important because her younger sister has recently died of cancer. Because so far she had only remembered the abuse memories from her childhood, she wanted to remember some good memories of her sister from that time.

The only thing is that she says she has had a history of terrible relationships, co-dependent, dysfunctional relationships. Currently, she was in a good relationship. She had been in it for a while and was getting married in a week. Her fiance knew about the abuse. He had never abused her and was sensitive to her sexual difficulties, but she still had fear right before they would have sex. During sex, she would usually dissociate, feel numb, or feel like a child. In the past she'd been really promiscuous, but always inside she was either really scared or numb or like a little girl. She had been in sadomasochistic relationships and was severely beaten one time by a man with whom she was living. It was then that she had decided to get sober and get out of the S/M life. Later, she became a therapist.

The presenting complaints are that she dissociates and becomes fearful around sexual activity, and she can't remember good times with her sister during their childhood. I think hypnosis is good for treating this stuff. The tape shows what we do. She's been in trance a number of times before through listening to self-hypnotic tapes and in practice sessions during the workshop.

BILL: Good, so you have been in trance before lots of times.

SUBJECT: Yeah.

BILL: Okay, good. So let yourself **go into trance**, and I am going to say in a way that is appropriate for you, safe for you, as safe as possible in this particular setting. To go wherever you need to go. To move yourself along towards those goals, towards resolving, towards remembering just as much as you need to remember and just as little as you need to remember.

I start the trance induction using what I call **encouraging and restraining** in the induction. I suggest that she go into the trance, which is encouraging, but I suggest she not go any deeper than is appropriate for her or remember more than she needs to. This approach is especially important in this public forum, to make sure that I don't intrude on her boundaries. That's what has happened during the abuse, somebody has intruded on her boundaries a lot. I want to make sure I don't intrude on her boundaries or force her to go anywhere experientially that she does not want to go. So I'm doing this restraining: "Remembering all you need to remember, forget all you need to forget. Don't go in any deeper than is appropriate for you." That encourages her to go into trance, but it's also protective. I trust her to know much better than I do what she needs to do.

BILL: And you may have already done all of the remembering you
need to do or want to do and somehow find a way to create the
room in there, the space in there for you to be **validated**, who you
are, how you are, for you to include your history, your experience,
the things you have done, the things that have been done to you.
To be able to **leave the then time in the then time**, and when you
are in the now time to be able to know about all the then time that
you need to know about as part of your background of **learnings**
and experience and to really be in the now time and to be able to
give yourself **permission** . . . that's right . . . to have felt the things
you've felt, and separate that from blame or approval, and find
some way to reconcile and connect in a way that is meaningful to
you the past to the present to the future and to disconnect any
parts that are not meaningful to you or useful for you. To know
about consciously and bring into the present and the future.

If she's good at dissociating and making splits, I might as well
provide possible splits that are good and healing. She wasn't initially making that distinction between the things that she had done
and the things that were done to her. So, I help her make that
distinction. I help her to organize her experience in a different way.
I'm going to propose several other splits as we go along.

BILL: As we've talked all day, you have abilities, skills, resources
and strengths, coping mechanisms, ways of dealing with things,
ways of not dealing with things, and you can just rearrange those
in any ways that you need to rearrange those. And your hand may
start to **lift up**. That may be one of those things you have done in
hypnosis before. It could **lift up** and as it starts to **lift up to your
face**, you can be doing the work that you need to do. It may be in
terms of **resolving**, and it may be in terms of remembering and
may be in terms of remembering to forget the things that are inter-
fering with your good memories. The memories you would like to
keep more present in the future.

What's she good at. Dissociating her body. So why hand levitation? Because it involves dissociation, something she already does
quite readily and well. Then I'll use that body movement, muscle

movement as a way to link dissociation to healing and to her emotions so that now her dissociation can lead to new, more useful associations.

BILL: As that **hand** continues to **lift up**, and it can **lift up to your face**, it doesn't have to, and it might be **lifting up to your face**. And as it **comes in contact** with your face, as it does, that can be the signal for you to do whatever it is that you need to do. To include within that work any emotions or experiences you have had and that you have, that you need to have, whatever you need to know, experience at the rate of that which you could know that. And you can **change time** to do that in a way that is right for you.

"Comes in contact" is a pun. When she's having sex she's not in contact. That can be a pun for when she's having orgasms she'll be in contact, rather than dissociated.

BILL: You can come **up** with something that lets you know that these **changes** have occurred. And when it is time in that process, as that hand continues, up toward your face, in an appropriate way you can find the resources you need to resolve that in a way that's right for you.

" . . . come up with something that lets you know that these changes have occurred." The hand lifting is used as a signal that these changes have occurred.

BILL: And after it touches your face you can at some time, when you are ready, maybe right away, maybe in a minute or two, three minutes, you can **open your eyes and look at me** when you are ready, and I'm going to talk to you just briefly and find out from you if there is anything that I need to know or what I need to know.

"After it touches your face," presupposes that it's going to touch the face. There's that illusion of alternatives: "It could be right away or maybe in two or three minutes."

BILL: Now is these anything I need to know or to tell you to do inside or to talk to you about while you are in trance? So what is happening right now?

SUBJECT: I see little boxes.

BILL: Little boxes?

SUBJECT: With the "then" and the "now," with a minus sign and an arrow taking all the hurtful experiences and leaving them and they kind of pass through the now and there was little like addition signs, and they were kind of shifting around the boxes, and they would superimpose on each other. And realizing that I am who I am because of them.

BILL: Right, and it has made in a weird way it has made a contribution to who you are. That is not all bad. It was good in a lot of ways. Okay, good.

I offered a reframing based on my experience that things that have been hurtful to me have ultimately been a contribution to me. The bad stuff can lead to good stuff now and in the future. If you transform it or learn from it, it can be a contribution.

She also tells me about a spontaneous visualization she's been having. She tells me a lot more of detail about this when she comes out of trance. What I suggested was that she could leave the past—the "then" time—in the past and be fully in the present and have the future be the future. I was helping her to distinguish those. Then, I suggested that she could connect the past, present, and future in a way that was meaningful for her. She saw a box into which she put all the hurtful experiences she had and all the poor sexual choices she had made. That represented the past. That box had a "−" sign on it, a negative sign. Then she had a box for the present that had a "+" sign on it, because things were going well in her current life. Then she had a "+" sign on the future because she expected things to go better in the future. When I suggested she connect them in a way that was meaningful, she saw the boxes superimpose on one another so they came with a "+" sign on the combined box.

I was just checking in with her to see if there was anything she needed to tell me 'cause we had such a short time I really wanted some oral feedback rather than just reading her body. I wanted to know if there way anything we needed to talk about. In retrospect it seems like a pretty good idea, because while she's pretty dissociated I have her open her eyes and make contact with me. Later, when she starts to dissociate with her husband before sex, she opens her eyes and tells him, "I'm dissociating and we need to slow down." So this little chat gave her some practice at learning to communicate when starting to dissociate.

BILL: All right, so you close your eyes and find a way to put those things in their place and have them be the platform on which you stand to see farther into the future, to step off into the future, in a **safe** way so that you can feel solid grounding underneath you. And, also, I think it would be nice while you are in that trance to be able to find a way to make arrangements with yourself to **be there for the pleasurable parts** when it is **safe** and when it is a situation that you trust, to **be there for the pleasurable parts of having sex**, when it's appropriate for you. To be able to be fully in your experience and to know that what happened then was then and it had all sorts of ramifications then, had all sorts of meanings for then and as you were growing up. With the resources you have now and the understanding you have now and that you are getting as moments **go on**, minutes, days, months, and weeks and years **go on**, that you could **come to a new understanding** and even appreciation **of your history**.

I'm linking the resources and the understandings to the present and to the future. I'm also marking out the words, "go on." In fact I'm writing up this case and I'm calling it, **"History Becomes Herstory."** Her life was lived out of this narrative, this story, based on what some guy did to her years ago. What I wanted to do was to give her back her own life story. So she could write her story. It was **his** story up to this point, and now it's **her** story.

BILL: I used to be real depressed and real shy and very miserable, and I think that kind of sensitivity to that kind of pain has been one of the things that has made me very sensitive as a therapist to other people's pain and discomfort, also to the possibilities of change. 'Cause with me, I thought I was a hopeless case and now I realize I wasn't a hopeless case and that somewhere deep inside I knew I would make it through. That somewhere deep inside there was a strength and resilience even in the midst of what looked like fragility to me, like I couldn't handle anything and that I couldn't deal with anything, and I was full of fear but I came to appreciate the sensitivity that gave me and to tap into the strengths. And that's one way I have come to appreciate the sensitivity that gave me and to tap into the strengths. And that's one way I have come to reconcile myself with those experiences and those hurts. I think it'd also be nice while you are in trance to really have something to come to your mind that's pleasant from your childhood, from your growing up, maybe something to do with your sister, I think that'd be nice. Maybe just a flash or maybe a full-blown memory or experience or maybe just a feeling. I remember my sister and I as we were little, climbing in the middle of a folded-away bed that was folded up, it was real tight and it felt like our fort. I don't really remember what it looked like or where it was, I just remember the feeling of that fold-away bed. And I think the body remembers those good feelings, too; in sort of a connection and a legacy that your sister's left behind in your experience, your feelings and memories of her.

Since she's had flashbacks before, I might as well use them. If she's had flashbacks of bad experiences, why not good memories? Also, many people who have been sexually abused have taught me they usually remember with their bodies first and with their minds later. So, I offered the possibility of remembering good feelings with her body, too.

BILL: Your sister, even though she is not around, probably influenced people that you influence, that you are in contact with and connection with through the spirit and the memory of her, through those feelings. And you can bring those forward into the present and the future as well. And have a little more choice about that. Now, in a minute, I am going to suggest that that hand either starts to drift down, or you can just put it down very deliberately, whatever is most comfortable for you. And that as it goes back down to your thigh—that's right—you can begin comparing to complete this experience in trance knowing that each trance experience completion is also the beginning of other things and the opening of other things. So do that in a way that's right for you. When you are ready to come all of the way out of a trance leaving behind in trance the things that are for trance. Good. Thanks.

SUBJECT: That was good. I saw her clearly.

BILL: That's great. Good. Good job.

SUBJECT: A good memory just came back.

BILL: That's nice. Okay. Good.

Following this short session, we had a brief discussion with the audience.

I asked her to send me a letter in a month telling me what she had gotten from the experience. I received this letter from her:

Dear Bill,

Just a short note to update you on my progress since our session in Miami, as a demonstration on the topic of adults molested as children. The first thing I noted was when my husband and I had sex on our honeymoon night one week after the seminar, the first chance we had to have sex all week with the family in for the wedding, was that I did not dissociate. I was able to feel the physical enjoyment of the sex happening at the moment without having to retreat. I have also noticed an increase in my sex drive and a total distinguishing of my pre-sex fears. All my goals were accomplished automatically. Although I did not remember a lot of what you said specifically while in trance, I do remember you saying you used to be shy and depressed. I remember thinking for days later, "He used to be shy, wow! It sure doesn't show. I haven't written a letter to my abuser yet [*which I suggested she might*] but I will. I'm still floating in marital bliss. My deepest thanks for fitting me in and rearranging your syllabus.

I've kept in touch with her since then. She said that occasionally she would dissociate, but was able to tell her husband about it. Then they would talk or just stop or go slower or skip it that night.

But that most of the time she was not dissociated during sex with him. I thought this was a pretty good effect for such a short trance. You've also got to remember that she had been in a seminar for three days in which she felt really validated, and she was learning a lot of these skills while doing trances like you have been. I thought this was a nice example to illustrate how trance can do things automatically. She told me that she had to go back into her practice that week and got married the next weekend, so she didn't have time to think about what we did at all. That's the point of hypnosis. You don't have to consciously think about it to resolve this stuff. Somehow we are stimulating these unconscious processes so that you can be doing some work automatically. Obviously this a fairly straightforward case, she's pretty high functioning, cooperative, and easy to work with, but it shows the principles.

> AUDIENCE: If trust is such an issue with the survivors of sexual abuse, do you feel that you could as effectively work with someone with a conversational induction?

I don't usually. I let them know we are doing trance, partly because of an ethical stance of mine, but that's just me. I suspect with some people you might need to do a conversational induction. Or you might need to make adjustments. Steve Gilligan told me he was working with a woman who was totally freaked out about the possibility of trance. He usually does trance having people keep their eyes open as opposed to having their eyes closed, because he thinks sometimes people avoid relationships by escaping into a solitary trance. It was so scary for her to do this, so they worked out a method that made it tolerable for her. He would be in the middle of the office, and she would sit in the doorway, half in the room and half out of the room. That's the closest they could be at first when they did trance.

Gradually, as they progressed, they could move closer and closer. So, with anyone, but especially with sex abuse survivors, you have to let them teach you, by their responses, what is comfortable for them. If you find out they freeze up with a formal induction, the a conversational induction might be best. I wouldn't do that without getting their permission first, letting them know you were going to use trance sometime in the process of therapy. My experience is just the opposite, though. I've found that most people who have been abused are extremely good at going into trance because they spent much of their life in trance. They are naturally good. If they don't trust you, they are very good at staying out of trance, and I think they should, it's a good plan.

AUDIENCE: Do you always use the word trance or . . . ?

I use "hypnosis" or "trance." They'll find brochures that use those words in my waiting room, and it doesn't create problems for me. It may create problems for some people in some settings, so I don't think you need to be attached to that word. You might use "front of your mind," "back of your mind," or "one part of you" and "another part of you," "going deeper inside," "finding the resources within," or whatever you can come up with that makes sense for you and them. But, to me, it is all trance. Look, I work in Omaha, Nebraska, and somehow people in Omaha go for it, and they aren't the most sophisticated people in the world in regards to hypnosis.

AUDIENCE: Is there some kind of written release?

If one is very paranoid, one should have a written release for anything you do. I never had any trouble with it. The only legal warning I would give is that hypnotically derived testimony is not accepted in most states of the Union. It has really been pretty conclusively shown that hypnotically derived memories can be influenced by the hypnotist, the investigator. Sometimes if you hypnotize somebody who testifies in court later, their testimony might be thrown out because it *might* have been hypnotically influenced. If you are going to do that kind of investigation, I recommend videotaping it and following certain procedures. The FBI can give you the procedures to follow. Other than that, I haven't had any trouble with it. It's like any therapy procedure. Somebody could accuse you of doing something unethical or harmful, but if you act ethically and you have good relationships with your clients, it probably won't happen. But, if it did happen, if you've acted ethically and taken good case notes, you could defend yourself in court.

You can use this model to generate specific interventions — what is needed for *this* particular person. I want to get a specific problem focus and intervention plan, not something general like "working through the aftereffects of sexual abuse." For each individual, you have to figure out what *he or she* does. What are *their* aftereffects of sexual abuse? It's very specific to them. Now, after working with a number of people you can get some generalizations, but you still have to find out what are *this* person's goals? What are *this* person's goals that you are working with right now, what is *this* person's goal and how can you construe it as a class of problem, class of solution — then, how can you evoke it?

What specific automatic things did the woman on the tape *do* as part of her problem? One of the things she did was amnesia, and what's the doing of amnesia? Forgetting certain things automatically. Since she had already remembered the abuse memories in flashbacks, she might remember things in flashes. She might remember things in feelings. I want to use those resources, evoke those resources by telling stories. One of my stories was about me remembering something about my childhood and my sister. You may have noticed that it was a story about positive and good feelings associated with the bed. My sister and I were crawling in the middle of a fold-away bed that I said that it felt like our fort, really safe and really good. So the story had to do with a place where you could have safe and good feelings, safe and good memories. She then transferred it to the problem context, and she had a good memory of her sister. That was one of the things I was working on with her. The other one was to be associated rather than dissociated. So, we worked on dissociation leading to association and healing and good memories.

AUDIENCE: I kept thinking while you were telling these stories, maybe half of my cases I feel like I'm helping and the other half I don't know what I'm doing. I wonder, do you

find you still have cases you don't know what to do with or
they don't work out? Do you feel like every case works good
now?

Well, not every case works well, but I have a pretty clear sense
of what's going on in each case. It just doesn't always work. I can
say that I've moved through three phases in my career so far. The
first one, and the one I was joking about with Sharon is like, you
get out of graduate school and you go into a room, and they send
a client in there and you think, "Who? Me? I'm supposed to do this
work? I don't know what I'm doing and they are sending this
person!" You get real worried about it. You have this beginner's
mind, and you think, "I don't know what I'm doing and they are
paying me money for this and I'm supposed to know." Especially if
you get a really unusual case like a cult victim or somebody who is
anorexic, and they may die while they are in treatment. You think,
"They sent somebody into my office who, if I say the wrong thing,
may die. I don't know what I'm doing; they shouldn't send these
people into my office."

Then, at a certain point, you get enough experience and enough
models, you feel a certain confidence. So I got to a place where I
was, like, "Hey, no problem, I can handle anything." They can
send me all these people and I was sure I could solve anything. I
became an expert.

Then, I popped out of the expert mode into the beginner's mind
again. The standard joke I have is that it is too bad my clients
don't come to my workshops, because then they would know how
they are supposed to respond and get better when I use my clever
techniques and ideas.

I've found that my clients are always more varied than any
model I ever have. They teach me when it doesn't work. It almost
always does, and then sometimes it doesn't. I pop out of any model
that I learn into the beginners mind again. That term is from the
Zen saying, "In the expert's mind there are few possibilities and in
the beginner's mind there are many." I pop out into beginner's
mind again, and I figure I don't know anymore. But this time it's a
comfortable not knowing. Like, "I don't know, but we'll figure it

out together." I rarely get so lost that I think, "Oh, my God, I don't know what I'm doing, I don't know how to handle this."

Someone came in one time and said, "Do you treat cluster headaches?" I said I had never heard of cluster headaches. He said they were like migraines but much worse. He said, "They call them 44-caliber headaches." I asked why. He said, "Because you feel like shooting your brains out when you have them." It turns out they are like migraines that happen three or four times a day, or every day for six months or a year. He taught me about them, and I figured, "I don't know a thing about them. But if you teach me how you do a cluster headache, I'll have some pretty good ideas and then I'll start to experiment. Together we will figure out how to treat them." Like that. Same thing with the first person who came in that was abused by a cult. I didn't have a clue. I had read about it a bit, but I didn't have a clue, but she taught me how to work with her, and she coached me very, very well.

One time, somebody asked Erickson, "With all your great therapeutic skills and communication skills, do you think you could work with the situation in the Middle East and help that?" And he said, "Bring them to my office." I think the same thing. I can't tell you the solutions to every problem, but you bring the person to my office, and I'll find possibilities for them. It doesn't always work out, but I will find openings and possibilities, and I'll find ways to construe their problem that makes sense. I rarely get so lost that I can't find ways to think about their problem that are helpful, but that doesn't mean I always solve the problems.

AUDIENCE: How about if they just decide to leave?

Yeah, one way or another, my brilliant ideas don't always translate across to their experience. That's that.

AUDIENCE: It's always like that, I guess.

I think it is. You know, when I was in high school I went to a health education class that was really freeing for me because the lecturer said, "95% of males masturbate . . . and 5% lie." That made me feel a lot better. It's the same thing with therapy. I think if anybody claims 100% success rate, they are the 5% that lie. I want to watch their work for a long time. What are they defining as success, collecting the fee or what? Or is it lasting results over a long time? I don't know anybody who gets 100% success rate, although I've heard some people claim it. I've been to their seminars.

> AUDIENCE: If in the midst of a trance you decide that you want to have some dialogue, it looks like you generally have the clients open their eyes.

Generally, not always.

> AUDIENCE: Are there some other general principles about having dialogue during trance?

I don't usually have dialogues. I don't usually have people talk to me, partly because I think their bodies are communicating to me. Their bodies coach me in what I'm supposed to say, and I get a lot from just watching them and not having a lot of thoughts. Also, using this solution-oriented model, we aren't searching for a lot of explanations or looking for hidden and repressed material, so I don't need clients to tell me a lot of things orally. I'm just offering possibilities and, like in curling, sweeping right in front of them, saying in effect, "How about this, you want to do this? Is this going to be a helpful experience?" To mix my metaphors, I'm offering them a smorgasbord of possibilities. I spend a lot of time talking because I'm really trying to create some experience for them. Sometimes I'll do a lot of dialogue back and forth if they coach me that that's what they want to do.

It is partly a manner of style, too. You just get used to doing trance a particular way. I learned a lot from Erickson, who mainly dominated the conversation while doing trancework. But, if somebody wants to talk when they go into trance or keep their eyes open the whole time, you'd better allow for that and not have this response of "I learned it in the workshop—you are supposed to keep your eyes and your mouth closed." Then that becomes your limitation.

> AUDIENCE: Have you ever had anybody who was scared when they were in the middle of trance? It must be scary, bringing up some memories and things that they. . . . How do you handle that, do you have to stay with it or . . . ?

When I first went to hypnosis workshops, they kept saying this thing that really scared me: "Beware of the abreaction." Abreaction is a fancy word for freaking out. They taught me all sorts of techniques to get people out of the abreaction. I was always a bit wary for about the first five years when I was doing trancework. I kept wondering, "Where's the abreaction? Maybe I'm just not doing it right, since I'm not getting a lot of it." After a while, I realized that what they meant wasn't what I was thinking. I thought the client would maybe bounce off the ceiling or bounce off the wall. What *they* meant was that sometimes people cry in trance and sometimes people get upset, laugh hysterically, or get really scared. I thought, "Well, that's abreaction? That doesn't bother me." I used to work in the area of crisis counseling and people would come in all the time freaked out. In outpatient counseling people freak out all the time. Finally, I demystified it for myself with this rule of thumb: When people are in trance, treat them as if they are normal. I know it's a strange and difficult concept to grasp, but think about it this way: If the person is in trance and starts crying what would you do if they weren't in trance and started crying?

> AUDIENCE: Give them a tissue.

Give them a tissue. Or you might ask, "What are those tears about?" Or, "Is it okay for you to cry? Do you want to tell me anything about that?" What if somebody doesn't come out of trance? That's another question I often get. First of all, remember to demystify it for yourself. There is nothing that they are "in." They are just sitting in a chair, and you are having a conversation. They are not "in" anything. It's just a metaphor. We often use spatial metaphors for mental processes and for trance. "Deep,"

"Go all the way in," these are depth metaphors. Don't take the metaphor literally. That's schizophrenia. Using my rule of thumb, if there is somebody sitting in a chair, and they have their eyes closed, and they are not moving a whole lot, and it's time to end the session but they still don't move or seem to respond when you talk to them, what would you do?

AUDIENCE: Stand up, move.

You would stand up and move, as a social signal, "It's time to leave." What if they still sat there when you stood up and moved?

AUDIENCE: Touch them.

I found that if you touch people who are in trance, it typically brings them out.

I might say, "Anybody home?" I often use humor. What would you do if they weren't in trance and they were doing the same behavior? That's the question. Because in trance they are not psychotic or not available to you, they are just having experiences. Sometimes they are very deeply involved in those experiences. What can you do to get them deeply involved in a conversation with you instead of their own internal experiences? Just what you would do with a regular client or a regular patient.

Any other questions? Is it starting to come together for you? (*Head nods*)

Exercise #5: Mutual Hypnosis

One more exercise, and we'll take a break. This exercise I really enjoy. It's one of my favorites. I got it from Steve Gilligan, who is an excellent hypnotist. I recommend that you go to one of his workshops sometime. This exercise will give you an opportunity to do what we call **mutual hypnosis**. Mutual hypnosis is when you each hypnotize each other sequentially. Again, speak when the person exhales. If I'm working with Tina, I'm going to say four or five hypnotic statements like, "You can sit there in the chair nodding, blinking, and listening to my voice, and you might start to tune in, and you might want to close your eyes if it's comfortable for you, but you don't have to close your eyes to go into trance. Letting yourself be exactly where you are. Consciously thinking what you are thinking, that's right, and unconsciously just allowing yourself to begin that process of going into trance, or to continue the process of going into trance." And after I get done with my four or five statements and I think she's responding really well, I'm gonna let her know it's her turn to talk to me by saying this phrase: "And you're fantastic." So I'm going to look Tina meaningfully in the eyes and say, "And you're fantastic."

Okay, so first, speak on the exhalation; second, the first speaker says five to ten hypnotic statements and ends with the phrase "And you're fantastic." Then, the listener becomes the speaker and replicates the whole process until he or she passes it back to the first speaker by saying, "And you're fantastic." For this exercise, I'd like you to keep your eyes open the whole time and maintain eye contact.

Now, the specific goal you are going for, both of you, is inviting the person to find an experience or symbol of comfort, safety, and security. The symbol could be a visual image or it could be a particular person. It could be a particular time of comfort, security, and/or safety. It might be a particular visual image, a particular feeling, or it might be a particular memory, person, object that they have. For one client of mine it was an afghan, a knitted blanket that the only person in her family who didn't abuse her gave her. She would bring it into sessions. She discovered that that would help to keep her safe when she was remembering things she needed to remember and deal with. Invite the person to go inside if you will and find, allow, not actively search but allow whatever might be an experience of comfort, security, and safety to come into their experience or into their minds. Take about 20 minutes—I'll walk around and observe to get a sense of how people are doing. Go back and forth as many times as you need to. I would prefer that you keep your eyes open the whole time but, at a certain time, one person may drop out and not talk anymore. If that happens, take the wheel and just finish the exercise. Remember to say, "And you're fantastic" as a cue that the ball is over in their court, and they are supposed to talk to you now. If you wear glasses you should keep your glasses on for this experience unless you can see really well without them. So do that **now**.

(*The participants do the exercise.*)

Time to come back. What was that experience like for you? What did you learn? What did you bump up against? What useful experiences did you have? How many people experienced visual distortions like tunnel vision or auras or whatever? (*A number of participants raise their hands.*) All right. What? You do that all the time anyway? (*Laughter*)

AUDIENCE: All of a sudden I experienced a complete blank for a hypnotic phrase. I know I've heard bunches of them but all of a sudden I couldn't think of one.

Somehow you muddled through, though?

AUDIENCE: I must have.

"And you are sitting there in a chair and you're fantastic." (*Laughter*) And Wayne went, "Oh, it's my turn again."

AUDIENCE: I was selfish, from the group back here I caught, "And you're wonderful," and I thought, "Okay, I *am* wonderful," and then I came back.

Riding on somebody else's phrases, huh? And your partner was saying really profound things. I overheard her as I walked by. You missed all that great stuff she said.

AUDIENCE: The experience I had was strange. I didn't like having my eyes open as much as I liked having them closed. So my thinking is that I did a lot more conscious paying attention to stuff, and I'm not as aware of whatever I was creating unconsciously, but I got this sense of "I'm going to trust it anyway." I probably did something.

AUDIENCE: I had this sense of a twitch in the left arm, and I wanted her to ask me about it. This one kept twitching, but this one felt so heavy I couldn't lift it. It was a great experience.

We are going to do another exercise before the seminar ends about having the person coach you orally, but I wanted you to really tune into reading their body because most of us are most attuned to oral feedback and oral comments. I really wanted you to tune in to *physical* communications the person is giving through their hand twitches or whatever. In the next exercise we'll have you ask and get some oral comments back.

AUDIENCE: I was so self-conscious to have him staring at me. I could see my reflection off his glasses.

Looked as if he was looking at you with those fish eyes.

AUDIENCE: One experience I had was that it's easier to do a trance when I'm in trance myself.

Part of the purpose of this exercise was that. For some people, coming up with hypnotic phrases happens a lot easier if they are in trance, too. Also I wanted you to have an experience of being in trance and being externally focused, which is part of how I do the trances I do up here and in my office. It's also part of how most of you do therapy. You are externally focused and you are doing therapy in your therapy trance. Okay. What else?

AUDIENCE: I don't think I was in a kind of a trance.

For you it may not have facilitated trance. The interruption of going back and forth may have kept you out of trance. Thinking about those phrases and trying to come up with them interfered for you.

AUDIENCE: I was frustrated, because we got the cue words to keep going, and there was a part of me that was aware that I couldn't go as far as I really wanted to go, because I was needing to be ready any moment to go into action. And I found that frustrating.

Right, you never really let go as much because you were anticipating having to talk.

AUDIENCE: I was definitely in trance sort of, I could feel it but not as deep.

Well, that was different from your experience, Dennis, because for you it was a lot easier to be in trance and receiving and talking.

AUDIENCE: I don't know if I did better but one of the things that happened was my internal criticism of "You're not doing this very well," that sort of stopped.

Right. As you went into trance, that was not intruding in such a way as it used to, which was for me, the structure of shyness. I just had my inner Howard Cossell accompany me in life every place, commenting on my experience: "That's a dumb thing. Don't do that. You look dumb today," or whatever. That's how I did it.

AUDIENCE: It's getting easier to deal with someone whose eyes are open because I got in touch with the fact that I was more comfortable with their eyes closed, like they are not watching for my mistakes. It became okay.

You began trusting yourself and them a little more.

AUDIENCE: I think if I were doing this in my office and somebody had their eyes open, I would go into trance, it would feel more, because of the fixed look, like an automatic cue for me.

I go very, very deeply into trance when I work with people sometimes. That's one of the reasons I wanted you to do this exercise—to help you arrange to have your professional resources available even when you are in trance. Okay? Good. Let's take a break. When we come back, we'll be focusing on pain control and working with somatic difficulties.

SEVEN

Treating Pain and Somatic Problems

Now, we're going to address pain and somatic problems. I want to play you a couple of examples, then have you do some work. First, we're going to play the audiotape of Joe Barber. And the nice part about Joe Barber's work, and this is one thing that we will have you practice, is that he does a lot of what we call **interspersal**—a lot of the marking out of words. You'll hear him mark out certain words. He'll be saying the word "attention" and he'll mark out the part of it that says "tension." And then he'll mark out "comfort," he'll mark out "relaxed." So, tension, relax—tension, relax. You might want to participate in this experientially. That is, you might want to close your eyes and settle in as he suggests to do and just participate in this experientially. Or you might want to just read the transcript and follow along, it's pretty clear. I'll probably be pointing out a few things here and there.

Audiotape Example #3: Joseph Barber— Interspersal for Pain Control

I would like to spend the next few minutes talking with you in order to see just how **comfortable** and **relaxed** you may want to feel. Now, it would be nice if you would let yourself

166

settle back right now and get as comfortable as you can. Just settle back in whatever way is most comfortable for you right now without having to do anything special about that and without expecting anything special about that. But just let yourself settle back and you might like to put your hands at your sides or on your lap. You might want to let your feet just stretch out and relax. And as you rest back, I'd like you just to begin noticing what it is that you're feeling now. And perhaps notice in what ways your experience changes from moment to moment. And as you continue hearing what I'm saying to you, I'd like you just to let yourself begin breathing easily and comfortably and I would like you to pay particular attention to your breathing. For right now, I'd like you just to pay attention to your breathing and just notice the feelings associated with your breathing. Notice for instance, that when you breathe in, there's a different quality to the physical sensations in your chest. Notice as you exhale how those physical sensations change. And as you breathe in again, feel the air coming in to your body and filling your lungs. And as you breathe out, feel the warmth of the air leaving you comfortably and easily. And there isn't any particular way that you need to breathe right now. I want you just to notice your breathing and to pay particular attention to the feelings associated with every breath you take. And as you continue, I'd like you just to let your eyelids close all the way and let them just stay closed. So that with your eyelids closed, you can continue paying attention to your breathing. And to notice the physical sensations associated with every breath you take. And as you continue, I'd like you just to notice, just to notice if as you continue, each time you exhale, you might feel a little more relaxed. Each time you exhale, I wonder if you noticed that you might feel a kind of warmth across your back and your chest. A very pleasant kind of warmth, a very natural kind of warmth. This can occur as you allow yourself to relax and allow your blood vessels to relax and to allow your blood to flow freely and easily all through your system. So that it's almost as if your body is just beginning to rest almost is if you're beginning to rest. Resting back with your

eyes closed. Breathing easily and allowing yourself to notice
your experience from one moment to the next. And as you
continue, I want you to know that you don't have to listen to
what I'm saying to you. You will **hear everything** I'm saying
to you, that's inevitable. Because you have good ears and I'm
speaking loudly enough and clearly enough. But you really
don't have to listen to what I'm saying to you. At one level
you can hear what I'm saying to you—you hear the sound,
but you don't have to listen, you don't have to pay attention
if you don't want to. You don't need to. Your unconscious
mind is hearing everything I am saying to you. So there's
really no need for you to consciously pay any attention at all.
Consciously you might enjoy letting your mind wander and
drift. Consciously, you might enjoy a pleasant daydream
about something that you have enjoyed doing in the past. Or
you might prefer to enjoy a pleasant fantasy about something
you would like to do in the future. Or maybe you want to
listen carefully and critically to what I'm saying. I don't know.

Now we are going to go onto another one that will introduce a
lot more in terms of specific pain control techniques. By the way,
the only thing I would correct about what Joe Barber said, that I
found a little intrusive, was when he said, "You will hear everything that I say because you have good ears." Not everybody thinks
they have good ears, and not everybody has good ears. That would
be intrusive for me.

Audiotape Example #4: Milton Erickson—
Treatment of Tinnitus and
Phantom Limb Pain

Next is an edited example of one of Erickson's therapy sessions. In
this session he works with a couple. The husband has phantom
limb pain and she has tinnitus, ringing in the ears. The phantom
limb pain is that the husband has gotten a limb removed, but he
still feels pain in it. Which you may get in the spinal cord injury
field sometimes. Mainly when people have had amputations and
they still feel pain in a leg or an arm that isn't there or an arm that

isn't there. It feels at times that the arm is being twisted behind their back, but there's no arm. It's cut off. So, he has this experience. You might think, "Well, okay, sounds pretty good, he could do pain control with him." The guy has phantom limb pain, woman has tinnitus. So that's the specific complaint. Let's go to the class of problems/class of solutions. What's the same about both of them? Erickson's going to work with both of them at once. One way to construe it is the class of problems as **noxious sensory stimuli**. That is, they both have something in their sensory fields that is pretty noxious.

You might say "noxious imaginary sensory stimuli" because he feels a feeling in his leg when his leg isn't there, and she hears this noise in her ear when there's no noise present. Let's just call it "noxious sensory stimuli" and then one class of solutions is you could tune out constant noxious sensory stimuli or the more formal name in hypnosis is **negative stimulation**. Then what Erickson is going to do is give a bunch of specific things, some anecdotes, and later he's going to do hypnosis to evoke the ability that each of them has to tune out constant noxious sensory stimuli. Now he uses several other classes of problems, classes of solution with this, but I've just picked out mainly the ones that are of this particular variety. So you can follow along and, again, I've edited out a lot of stuff. Initially the woman says, "Well this phantom limb pain, that's the main thing, if we could lick that, that would be great." Then Erickson starts right in telling stories.

WIFE: Well this phantom limb pain—if we could lick that, it would be wonderful.

ERICKSON: All right. Now I'm going to give you a story so that you can understand better that we learn things in an unusual way, a way that we don't know about. In my first year of college I happened to come across that summer a boiler factory. The crews were working together on 12 boilers at the same time, three shifts of workmen. And those pneumatic hammers were pounding away, driving rivets into the boilers. I heard that noise and I wanted to find out what it was. On learning that it was a boiler factory, I went in, and I couldn't hear anybody talking. I could see the various employees were conversing. I could see the foreman's lips moving, but I couldn't hear what he said to me. He heard what I said. So I had him come outside so I could talk to him. And I asked him for permission to roll up in my blanket and sleep on the floor for one night. He thought something was wrong with me. I explained that I was a premedic student and that I was interested in *learning* processes. And he agreed that I could roll up my blanket and sleep on the floor. He explained to all the men and left an explanation for the succeeding shift of men. The next morning I awakened. I could hear the workmen talking about that damn fool kid. What in hell was he sleeping on the floor there for? What did he think he could learn? During my sleep that night I blotted out all that horrible noise of the 12 or more pneumatic hammers, and I could hear voices. I knew that it was possible to learn to hear only certain sounds if you tuned your ears properly. You have ringing in the ears, but you haven't thought of tuning them so that you don't hear the ringing. . . . And you can get so used to the ringing in your ears that you don't hear it.

Now so far you think, "Okay, what is this about? Maybe it's good treatment for the wife but they mainly came there for the husband for the phantom limb pain." You can see that using the class of problems/class of solutions that it's the same class of problems/class of solutions. He's seemingly working with her, but he's also talking to this guy: "You can do the same thing" essentially is the message.

> AUDIENCE: Do you think there is any reason why he chose her instead of him to start with?

Well I think if you listen to the whole tape it's pretty clear she runs the show. That may have been one of the reasons. He liked to work indirectly, that's another reason. To bypass that resistance, that conscious sort of processing of things. If Erickson's telling these stories for this woman, the man doesn't have to think, "Oh, I can't do that," or "That won't work for me." He's just going to be very interested, "Oh, that's interesting. She can learn to tune out her tinnitus." And all the while the husband's learning experientially as well. So maybe that's the reason. I really don't know for sure, maybe he just found an elegant way to work with both of them and that was a good way to start. Later, he does point it a little more to the husband. So he starts to tell more stories. Several other little analogies or anecdotes.

ERICKSON: On the "Tribal Eye" program on KAET, those nomads in Iran.* How can they dress with all those petticoats and be comfortable in the hot sun on those desert plains?

Okay, that was analogy or anecdote number two. The first one was the one about the boiler factory, now it's these Iranian tribesman in the hot desert sun. They wear a lot of clothes, and they are comfortable, but how can that be? Of course, they learn to tune the heat out, because it's constant.

ERICKSON: I grew up on the farm. I had to be away from the farm for quite some years before I learned the barn smell on your hands when you live on the farm. I never smelled it when I was on the farm. I had to be away from it for a long time before I discovered the barn smell. . . .

Analogy and anecdote number three. That barn smell on your hands, it's around all the time so you don't notice it, but if you go away from the farm and come back, you notice. Erickson later says, "I wondered how long it would take me to lose that barn smell? It took till mid-afternoon." That's an indirect suggestion of how long it will take them to get rid of their pain.

ERICKSON: What people don't know, that they can lose that pain. They don't know they can lose that ringing in the ears. When I discovered that that barn smell had come back, I could really smell it. I wondered how long it would take me that day to lose it. Then by mid-afternoon I couldn't smell it.

*This refers to a program on Phoenix's local public television station.

The Lanktons have suggested in several of their books to tell stories and stop the stories in the middle, giving some suggestions and then going back and finishing the stories as a way to induce amnesia for the suggestions we give people so that the suggestions are more likely to be processed by the unconscious. Here's an example of that. Erickson tells the beginning of the barn smell story, comes back and says, "People don't know that they can lose that pain, that noise," and then he goes back and tells the end of the barn smell story.

ERICKSON: All of us grow up believing that when you have pain, you must pay attention to it. And believing when you have ringing of the ears that you must keep on hearing it. . . . I'm talking to you while he is learning something.

He talks about a conscious belief people have about that. Talks about reframing that. "I'm talking to *you* while *he* is learning something." Again he's talking to the husband, linking over to the husband's experience by implication.

ERICKSON: He doesn't know what he is learning, but he is learning. And it isn't right for me to tell him, "You learn this or you learn that!" Let him learn whatever he wishes, in whatever order he wishes. . . .

"He doesn't know what he's learning, but he's learning." That's presupposition. Before he just attributed it, now he's presupposing.

ERICKSON: Now suppose you lean back and uncross your legs. Look at that spot there. Don't talk. Don't move. There is nothing really important to do, except go into a trance. You have seen your husband do it. And it is a nice feeling.

"Don't talk, don't move." That's pretty direct. By now he's gotten a bunch of responses by telling all these stories, she's ready to go into trance.

ERICKSON: Your blood pressure is already changing. You may close your eyes now and go deeper and deeper into the trance. You do not have to try hard to do anything. You just let it happen.

"You can close your eyes, *now*." That sounds pretty permissive, but it's pretty directive.

ERICKSON: And you think back; there are a goodly number of times this afternoon when you stopped hearing the ringing. It is hard to remember things that don't occur. But the ringing did stop. But because there was nothing there, you don't remember it. Now the important thing is to forget about the ringing and to remember the times when there was no ringing. And that is a process you learn.

Okay, now he's pointed out that in their experience sometime in that day, she's experienced tuning out noxious sensory stimuli. That's the solution-oriented approach. He's not going back and speculating about why he has pain and she has ringing in the ears, and searching for what function it serves in their marriage. Instead he is finding examples in her experience or creating examples in *her* experience of tuning out noxious sensory stimuli, and then creating those kinds of experiences for *him*. In another part of the session, he'll do a formal trance with the husband and amplify the evoked ability to tune out pain.

Next he goes back and finishes the story he started earlier, one of the first stories. The Lanktons called this **multiple embedded metaphor.** A bunch of stories are embedded within each other and a bunch of suggestions are embedded in the middle of those stories.

ERICKSON: I learned in one night's time not to hear the pneumatic hammers in the boiler factory—and to hear a conversation I couldn't hear the previous day. The men had been told I had come in the previous evening, and I talked to them and they kept trying to tell me, "But you can't hear us, you haven't gotten used to it." And they couldn't understand. They knew I had only been there a short time—one night—and they knew how long it had taken them to learn to hear conversations. They put their emphasis upon *learning* gradually. I knew what the body can do automatically. Now rely upon your body. Trust it. Believe in it. And know that it will serve you well. . . .

The moral of this story is that the unconscious mind can learn quicker than the conscious mind. The body can learn quicker than you can learn deliberately. Automatic learning is what he's looking for and pointing towards.

ERICKSON: You can go into a trance, I suggested, by counting to 20, and awaken by counting backward from 20 to 1, but each person should go into a trance in the way he *learns* naturally by himself. And you have *learned* an excellent way, and it's your way and be pleased with it and be pleased with extending the usefulness of that trance in many different ways. You both can learn from each other. And you can *learn* without trying to *learn*. There are so many things we *learn* from others, and we don't know we are *learning*. And our main, very difficult learnings we achieve without *knowing* that we are achieving those learnings. And you both are very responsive people. Which in less technical language means you both can *learn easily* things about yourself and *learn* them without needing to know that you have learned them. That you can use those learnings without needing to know that you know those learnings.

Now he's talking to the husband. He taught him a counting technique for going into trance.

ERICKSON: I am going to ask both of you to awaken gently and comfortably.

HUSBAND: Doctor, I'll say this. This has done as much good as that other one has done. This is going to be wonderful.

ERICKSON: You'll be surprised at all the new learnings that both of you will develop.

WIFE: Good, good.

ERICKSON: We will call it a day.

Okay, what comments questions or observations do you have on that taped example?

AUDIENCE: Had she given him information about having periods of freedom from ringing or was he assuming it?

No, I think he was assuming that and presuming that. Later, she talks about some experiences that he uses in a different way that are related to other pleasant experiences she's had with her ears. She remembers teaching a little retarded kid piano. Her husband remarked, "I think she enjoyed those lessons more than the little boy did," and Erickson has her remember the music that the retarded kid played in place of the ringing, but I don't think she'd told him anything specific about periods of relief from the ringing.

AUDIENCE: I don't know any thing about that disorder so I don't know if it ordinarily has periods where there's no ringing.

I've treated it a few times and people have told me that there are periods when it goes away or fades into the background.

AUDIENCE: So that was a safe assumption on his part on not intruding into her experience.

Right, it was a pretty safe assumption. The same thing happens with pain. People report it as constant, but if you actually get very specific, there are moments when they don't notice it or don't experience it.

AUDIENCE: Well, he also put a double bind to it, "When you are without it you wouldn't remember because you were without it." Like you never did have it.

Yes, it would be very difficult to note the ringing when it wasn't there. That was pretty clever, I thought. She starts to become convinced because he makes it pretty compelling logically as well as experientially. Probably at some time in that session she had lost it, because she was in and out of trance. I've often found that when people go into trance, they do lose the ringing in their ears or they do lose their pain for at least some of the time. This is one of the very few examples we have of Erickson actually doing therapy on tape, because most of the time the tapes involve demonstrations. But this was a couple that came to him for treatment and was recorded. It's nice to have because it illustrates this model quite well. He was working to evoke certain abilities, resources and skills. To do that he told a bunch of anecdotes and analogies and then did a trance induction to amplify the evoked experience.

That example leads us into examining the use of trance for pain control and treating somatic problems. This is a handout (7.1) listing strategies on pain control.

Typically, there are 11 strategies that I use for pain control. Usually the way I work is to go through a smorgasbord of these possibilities for people. Because, initially, I don't know which one or ones will be the most compelling or experientially useful for that person, I go down the list and offer them the smorgasbord. As they respond they start to teach me that one or two or three are going to be useful for them. And so they'll come back the next time and say, "I don't know, I just guess there were times that I forgot I had pain." They're teaching me that they responded to the suggestions for amnesia. Or they'll say, "I had pain, but it was sort of distant from me." They're teaching me they used dissociation. Or they'll say, "I had some sensation there but it was sort of a tingling." They used the strategy of altering sensations. These are a bunch of strategies one can use, and they'll either show you right in the session that they are using them, they'll tell you after they come out of trance, or they'll tell you when they come back in for more sessions that they've experienced one or more of these particular methods of pain control. I start with a broad range of possibilities and then hone it down based on how the person responds verbally and nonverbally, right in the session and between sessions.

AUDIENCE: Do you think that for people who are using drugs a lot to control the pain, that there is a special way to deal with them?

Handout 7.1
STRATEGIES FOR PAIN CONTROL

1. **ANESTHESIA**—lack of feeling in all or part of the body

2. **ANALGESIA**—lack of pain in all or part of the body

3. **AMNESIA**—forgetting previous pain

4. **DISSOCIATION**—detaching conscious awareness or experience from some aspect of experience

5. **REINTERPRETATION**—changing the frame of reference or perception regarding the sensations of pain

6. **TIME DISTORTION**—expanding the subjective experience of time when the person feels more comfortable, condensing time when the person feels pain

7. **ALTERING SENSATIONS AND PHYSIOLOGICAL PROCESSES**—changing the sensations associated with pain (to tingling or coolness, for example) and/or changing physiological processes associated with pain (like muscle tension or blood flow)

8. **RE-EVOKING PAIN-FREE OR PAIN-INCOMPATIBLE MEMORIES**—getting the person involved in memories of more pleasant times or experiences or times when pain has been diminished or eliminated

9. **DISTRACTION OR ABSORPTION OF ATTENTION**—refocusing the person's attention on some experience other than pain

10. **DISPLACEMENT OF PAIN**—putting the pain in another location in the body or in the world

11. **CREATE A COMPELLING SENSE OF A PAIN-FREE OR PAIN-DIMINISHED FUTURE**—using presupposition, analogy, metaphor, age progression, and/or imagery (positive hallucination), get the person to open up the idea that the future holds the likelihood of less or no pain.

Erickson used to imply that, because he'd have people go off drugs for 12 hours before he'd do the hypnosis with them. I haven't found that drugs really affect the results one way or another for me. If they are so out of it they really can't pay attention and can't attend to what I'm saying at all, I think that would get in the way. If they are just drugged, but not out of it, I think they can get with it. I would try hypnosis anyway, even if they weren't willing to go off the meds. That's just my sense of it so far.

Make sure you put in protections for people. I said to Wayne yesterday, "Eliminate all the unnecessary discomfort. Anything that doesn't serve a signal value or that's not useful for you." I think that people will protect themselves automatically, you might as well put those precautions in, just to be on the safe side.

In terms of the somatic difficulties people have, I have a generic sort of model in addition to the specific one we've already detailed in the Class of Problems/Class of Solutions Model. Say someone comes in for migraine headaches. They'll go into trance, and I'll tell them while they are in trance, "You know, you're an expert at getting rid of migraine headaches. I've never gotten rid of a migraine in my life because I've never had one, but you've had a bunch of migraine headaches and gotten rid of them. Now you've told me that the medication really doesn't help eliminate the migraine headaches. So somehow, someway, those migraine headaches have gone away. Somehow, your body has been able to make changes; maybe it's made changes in the muscles, blood flow, body chemistry, or muscle tension. I really don't know what your body has done to eliminate the migraine headaches but, somehow, you've been able to do that. So what I'd suggest is the next time you start to have what would be a migraine headache, what I'd suggest is that you do the pattern of getting rid of migraine headaches right then. So, instead of going all the way through the headache, you might as well bring the pattern of getting rid of it right to the beginning of it and make those kind of physical, psychological, emotional changes, spiritual changes, whatever kind of changes happen, to eliminate the headache." I found that to be pretty consistently helpful for people with somatic difficulties. You know, I think the body has a wisdom to it, and what we are doing at that point is tapping into the body's wisdom. If I said, "How do you get rid of your migraine headaches?" they'd say, "I don't have a clue." But if you say, "But your body knows and your unconscious mind has access to that knowledge and can use that knowledge to help you in the future," you are empowering them and tapping into their healing abilities, their change abilities. That's the model I'd like to show you in the demonstration.

Demonstration #3: Treating Pain and Somatic Problems

I'd like to have two or three people again, sitting in a chair, who would like to go into a trance, regarding a pain issue. A chronic pain issue if they have one, an acute pain issue if they have that. Things like migraine headaches, cluster headaches, arthritis, or a somatic issue. It should be something you haven't been able to take care of through medical interventions so far, and you'd like to do some work on it here. Make some changes here. So who's got some of that stuff? All right there's one, two, come on up. (Bill's comments are in parentheses.)

BILL: I'm going to ask each of you, when this is over, as you get out of your chair and you walk away, how will you know that what we did really made a difference for you, really made a contribution and helped? You might not know for a week, or two weeks, or a month, but ultimately or interimly, either sitting in that chair or getting out of that chair or a week from now, a day from now or six months from now, how will you know that we really made a difference in what you came up here for?

SUBJECT 1: I have chronic arthritis in my knees and my knees ache. I'll be more comfortable going up and down the stairs.

SUBJECT 2: Tension headache and sinus headache that I have today.

BILL: So, you'd notice an immediate difference. Are those things that you have had chronically?

SUBJECT 2: Pretty often.

BILL: So, you might notice a difference also in the future, but you'd certainly be able to check right here when you get off that chair. You could really notice it being much different from when you came up here. Better, much different better.

SUBJECT 1: The pain in my cartilage will go away, and then also when I get up and down it won't hurt so much; this front part of it.

BILL: Okay. Good. So I'd say the best thing to do is get yourself ready to go into trance in the way that you do, take off your glasses. If you are going to close your eyes to go into trance, you can do that now. And if you open them as you go along, that's fine. It's really up to you. Initially you can just let yourself be exactly where you are, feeling what you are feeling, experiencing what you are experiencing. Not particularly trying to **relax or feel more comfortable** or make yourself **go into trance** . . . just letting whatever conscious distractions are there be there, whatever conscious efforts are there to be there . . . and letting yourself in your own way . . . start the process of **going into trance** in a way that works for you . . . maybe by remembering . . . previous trances you've been in here, or other trance-like experiences that you've had . . . and it might be that you begin to feel some of those processes . . . of **change** . . . **changes** in your perceptions, maybe an **alteration in your feelings,** sensations, maybe some of that alteration in your muscles of having that sense of **muscle relaxation** that you have sometimes with trance. Or that sense of the muscles being operated independently by your unconscious mind, by your body, dissociated with that, hand levitation, arm levitation, that automatic **lifting,** that process that you may have experienced before, that you experience again, as a way to evoke **deeper trance further your trance** . . . indicate to you, that you are in trance and because this issue is very compelling for you experientially, you really would like to **feel better, feel more comfortable,** eliminate all the unnecessary dis**comfort,** that **hand movement,** that **hand lifting** . . . can be linked to that **good feeling** of knowing that you can trust yourself to **go into trance** and to **let your unconscious work for you** and give you a clear signal that it can **come up** with the resources you need to **clear up** the difficulties, to open **up** the possibilities of change, to help you **feel better, more comfortable,** and really maybe even have **more fun.** And it can be kind of funny to have that **hand moving on its own, lifting on its own** . . . but it really has a serious purpose . . . and that purpose is to really give you access to your unconscious abilities to be able to **feel better, feel more comfortable,** now you could **change time** to help you **feel better, feel more comfortable** . . . **heal** . . . **change** . . . and you could stretch out the time that you **feel more comfortable** . . . **feel better.** . . . They say a watched pot never boils . . . and that means when you are really looking at something and watching it, it seems to take so much longer . . . and that could also be a resource for you, that you've been able to learn to **stretch out time** so that you have all the time that you need in there to make all the **changes** that you need to make. And I'm really not sure what those **changes** are. They could be perceptual **changes**. They could be **changes** in sensation. Did you ever live any place with a colder climate and go out without your gloves on? When you come back in your hands are feeling kind of **numb**, from the cold, and then you put your hands under a faucet, and you can't tell whether the water is warm or cold, because all you can do is notice this **strange sensation** that you really can't interpret right, 'cause the brain doesn't have enough information from the nerves to interpret it, so sensations are just sensations . . . until the brain interprets them . . . and that **interpretation can change** . . . just as you've **changed interpretations** of other things in your life. And sometimes in directive hypnosis people use the image of little colored switches in the brain, colored switches, that are the terminals or ends for the . . . nerve and you can switch off just the ones . . . the yellow ones, the blue ones or the red ones . . . the ones that are giving the **unnecessary signals** . . . the ones that aren't necessary for you, so in that traditional approach they say, "You should do that, you will do that." But I just say that you *could* do that, that that's one **possibility** . . . or sometimes it's like you grow so used to the **discomfort** that you develop calluses to the **discomfort**. . . . When I first started to play guitar, my fingers would hurt after a few minutes of playing guitar. Now I can play guitar for hours and my hands are **comfortable**. Part of that is that I developed calluses on the end of my fingers, so that I **feel more comfortable** playing **now**, and your nerves in a strange way and your synapses can develop calluses because they've become habituated to a certain level of sensation and, after a while, I guess it exhausts the chemistry of the synapses . . . and it just doesn't transmit the information any more because there is no news there . . . or sometimes it's like it takes a bigger sensation to jump across the gap, it's like a spark plug because it's been made bigger. You can gap your synapses in a different way, that's another **possibility**. . . . And how will you

first notice that you are **feeling more comfortable?** . . . that you're
feeling better? . . . what kind of **changes** will you notice **first?** Do
you think that anybody else will notice **right away?** Or will you
have to tell them about it? Will your conscious mind **notice?** Or
will it take a little while for your conscious noticing to happen,
and what will you be doing when this is no longer an issue for
you, when you've left it behind in the past? . . . and you're really
confident that your unconscious has been able to help you **feel**
better. Now will that hand **move up?** Even more? Will it stay
exactly where it is? Will it **lift up** to the face? Will it meander
around on its way up to the face? Or will it stay exactly where
it is? You don't know exactly consciously but you can find out
consciously as that **hand continues** . . . in its own way on its own
journey and you can just validate yourself for the response that
you are having while your unconscious mind is learning to uncover
your ability to **feel better, feel more comfortable** . . . to eliminate
the dis**comfort.** To **clear up** previous difficulties . . . to open **up**
. . . to what your unconscious knows and what will be useful for
you right now, to know . . . and to say yes to . . . or to say no to
. . . now there's nothing particular that you need to do to make
yourself **feel more comfortable,** although you could make some
conscious adjustments to **feel more comfortable,** the brain has the
ability, the mind has the ability, the body has the ability, to **make**
various alterations so that you can continue to **trust your body,** to
take care of what you need to take care of . . . to help you **feel**
better, feel more comfortable in a way that you don't need to know
about consciously, exactly how it happened, but that you can just
experience the results. Now, and in the future, just continuing on
your way towards a better sense of **well being** . . . of **health** . . .
of **healing** . . . and when that hand completes its journey, there
could be a pleasant surprise awaiting you . . . only you don't know
what that is consciously, although you may have some suspicions
and the conscious mind can doubt the results, doubt the response,
and it can continue to have those doubts, those skepticisms, those
thoughts, as you continue to develop the resources you need, to
feel more comfortable—to feel better now and in the future
. . . eliminate all the unnecessary dis**comfort,** evoke, experiences

of **comfort**, maybe of being on vacation, holiday or getting a back rub, getting a whole body massage, listening to music . . . and getting lost in the music . . . or smelling some of your favorite smells. I was talking at lunch, freshly baked bread is one of my favorite smells. It seems to flavor my whole experience when the house is filled with that smell. I have an automatic breadmaker that I can set so that I can wake up to that smell of freshly baked bread. That's a nice thing to wake up to. And how do you take care of yourself? And what are your pleasant associations? And good connections? That's right. Just continuing that activity at the unconscious level, at the bodily level and letting it go where it will . . . letting your unconscious give you a hand at **healing** and **feeling better**. And maybe you could see yourself in the future as it were the now, **feeling better, feeling good**, telling someone how you eliminated the dis**comfort** and what is was like and then feeling that image pull you towards it compellingly like a magnet . . . and knowing that I think your unconscious will protect you in any way that you need to be protected, physically, emotionally, psychologically, spiritually. . . . You can open yourself **up** to **new possibilities, changes, reorientations, new associations**, and now I'd like to one at a time, invite you to experience what Wayne experienced yesterday, and that is when I touch you just lightly, on the hand . . . to come out of trance from the neck up and you might listen to the other people talking and you might just drift away into your own thoughts or you might do both sequentially. So, one at a time, I'm going to ask you to have your body be in trance and to come out of trance from your neck up and ask you what you are experiencing now, or what you've been experiencing.

SUBJECT 1: I need to find my voice. I'm aware of the heaviness of my head. I'm glued here, stuck. (To the chair?) Uhum, and it's comfortable. (Comfortable. Good. Anything else?) No.

BILL: All right, that's fine. You can close your eyes and go all the way back into trance. What have *you* been experiencing?

SUBJECT 2: Floating, no real feeling, just heavy at the moment. And I noticed a change in my breathing, I became clear of where I can breathe and a feeling in my neck . . . feeling better already.

(Anything else particularly?) Yeah, the chair's hard. (The chair's hard, we maybe can do something about that when you go all the way back in, anything else?) (*Shakes head*)

BILL: Okay, you can close your eyes and go all the way back in, and I can tell you a couple of things. One thing that reminds me of when you said the chair was hard, was a time I did body dissociation. I had to use a secretary's office, and she usually didn't have people in her office for very long but she had a chair for salespeople or something like that. But I had to use that office one night, so a client and I had to sit in these chairs that were sort of rope chairs, sort of like a hammock but a little harder. And after about a half hour—it was the first time the client had ever been in trance and she came in for breathing difficulties associated with pregnancy, so I decided it would be a nice thing to have her experience a body dissociation since I was feeling the chair as being very **uncomfortable** after about 15 or 20 minutes. About a half hour into session, I suggested that her body could be dissociated and glued to the chair and that she could be **comfortable** in her body and her body could take care of that breathing in a way that she didn't need to know about consciously. All she could experience was the result. And it was interesting because for me the chair was so hard the whole hour but for her, she said it immediately became a lot more **comfortable**. I don't know whether that will happen with you but I think it could happen with you. And you could breathe easier knowing that your unconscious mind could make some of those **changes automatically**, So, just continue that, and I'll let you know when it's time to complete the trance.

Wayne, what are you experiencing, what have you been experiencing?

WAYNE: Um, hand feels heavy, cold a little. (The one that's up?) Uhum, both are numb, I feel more like I'm trying hard today. (Bit of an effort?) Yeah, thinking more about images of healing and what I may want to be doing in a couple of months and imagining myself playing tennis without pain and in my leg back without it hurting. (Doing a little more conscious processing today; all right, anything else in a particular? Okay, that's fine. You can close your eyes and go all the way back in trance.)

BILL: And now, at your own rate and your own pace, start to do what you need to do to complete this particular trance in a way that's right for you, at a rate and a pace that's right for you. Maybe make arrangements with yourself for in the future, while you sleep . . . when you dream or any other way to continue to work on . . . or maybe to leave in the trance what you need to leave in the trance. And so when you are ready just start to complete the trance, if you haven't already and have your hands go back down to the positions that they were before. Start to reorient your body in the chair and you being in your body sitting in the chair or wherever else you are. And return to the present time and present place in a way that's right for you . . . when you are ready to come all the way out of trance just open your eyes and re-orient all the way. . . .

All right. A couple of minutes of questions and questions and comments and then we will have you all do an exercise. Anything in particular any of you want to say right away or do you want to wait for a little while?

SUBJECT 1: I didn't want to come back to my body because when you were talking to him about the chair being hard, and the end of my spine was hating the chair, and I thought, "It might work for him but it's not going to work for me," and then it was like I wasn't sitting here, it just quit hurting. And when you said come back to your body I thought, "No, I'm not going to do that."

SUBJECT 2: I think I sort of lost it at the point where I had to talk.

BILL: Talking—yeah, that really brought you out a bit. I noticed that.

SUBJECT 2: Because before that I felt like my hands were just floating and also got kind of surround nothingness. I don't see images, but it's almost you can feel it in front of your face.

SUBJECT 1: One of the images I had at the end was taking a box with pain in it in the trance and leaving it and taking another box with the future images with the good ideas and putting that under my arm walking off.

BILL: That's a nice image. Okay, all right. Any questions or comments on that process, that experience? Did it have anything to do on the handout I gave you about strategies to use for pain control? Did you hear me do any of those or many of them? Good. I always like to demonstrate something that's relevant to what I am teaching.

SUBJECT 1: I don't have any idea what you said so somebody will have to tell me later.

BILL: It was profound and wonderful as usual. I don't remember what it was either, so somebody will have to tell me later. I'll be able to read the transcript later and think, "Wow, that was pretty good, I like that."

AUDIENCE: While you were doing that, I was taking a free ride of sorts but can you when you are in trance make your own decisions to do things? Like when you were doing that I wanted to see whose hand was doing what, but I had my eyes shut, and I thought "I won't open my eyes," and when I did that it was like, "oh wow" — my arms and legs were tingling, numb, and I went back down again.

BILL: I think you've answered your own question very adequately. Yeah, you make your own choices. And you could have come all the way out of a trance. You came partially out of a trance to look to be able to notice whose hand was up and then you went right back into it. I think people do make their own choices inside and that's real important. I'm not controlling people. Joe Barber has this joke, "If trance could control people I'd have this little army of people following me around doing stuff I don't want to be doing in life." I'm a good hypnotist but I'm not good at controlling people. I think people always have a vote on what they do. And regardless of whether you use trance or not. Controlling people is a different matter.

AUDIENCE: It felt like my fingers were touching each other funny. They felt funny but then when I went to try to consciously move them they were like numb. Like I was imagining that feeling or something.

BILL: Yeah. Okay, any other comments or questions?

AUDIENCE: Do you almost always have a hand or arm levitation occur whether you are directing or not?

BILL: No. And even if I direct it, I don't always have it occur, as we talked about before. But I think it's nice to do for the workshop, to get it so people can see that. It's nice to do for somatic difficulties because it involves automatic processes with the body. I always like it for that kind of thing. But I don't use it all the time for everything. Some people have never done it, and I've never suggested it to them. Other questions?

AUDIENCE: On one of the Erickson tapes Monde was doing a lot of smiling. These folks didn't seem to do that. Was there a reason for that?

BILL: Yeah, it wasn't very funny this time, but I think you saw that, in earlier demonstrations, sometimes I said something that was funny, and sometimes people would smile.

AUDIENCE: She seemed to do it not always in response to anything.

BILL: Right, sometimes she may have been feeling self-conscious. And then Erickson would use it and say, "That's right, it can be an enjoyable thing." I think people can smile and laugh in trance. I just don't think I was profoundly humorous this time.

SUBJECT 1: I noticed at one point I made a decision that I wanted to go deeper. I told myself I want to do that and when I did, it did.

BILL: You sort of took control of the process or influenced the process. It can be really a mixture of conscious and unconscious. You can consciously think, "I'd like to go deeper," and you might. Sometimes you'll think that, and you won't. It's really a mixture of conscious and unconscious processes sometimes, at times mainly one, sometimes mainly another.

SUBJECT 1: I noticed along with that I would start to attend to my hand, and when I would begin to think about that I would start to get into conflict. I didn't want to think about that so much. I wanted to attend to what you were saying or think about something else.

BILL: Right, I actually gave that suggestion, 'cause "a watched pot never boils."

SUBJECT 1: So I tried not to watch.

SUBJECT 2: Permission to leave. When you said that we were going to become conscious from the neck up I thought, "Oh gosh, when that happens I'm probably going to laugh because my hand's in the air," but that didn't matter.

BILL: That didn't matter for you at that point.

Exercise #6: Inviting Body Dissociation

I'd like you to do an exercise and experiment. This time I'd like you to include some of that verbal feedback I was talking about while having people go into trance. I'd like you to again speak on the exhalation. The second component, this time, is to invite them into trance, and the third component is to ask them after they get into trance to awaken from the neck up and tell you what they're experiencing. That word "experience" is important because it doesn't pin them down into feelings or visualizations or sensations or thoughts or anything like that. It's vague enough to give them maximum freedom for how and what they report.

Even before they come out of trance from the neck up, though, I'd also like you to ask them on an ongoing basis, "What are you experiencing, and what have you been experiencing?" so that you can guide the process based on their comments. What I mean by that is you'll say a bunch of hypnotic things and then you'll say, "What are you experiencing right now?" Don't ask them to come out of the trance from the neck up. Just ask them, "What are you experiencing?" If they say, "I'm seeing colors," then you start back in based on what they've just told you. "You are seeing colors, and maybe you could see even more colors, and those colors could lead to other things and to you going deeper into trance." Just link to what they tell you. If they say, "I'm having a conflict about my hand going up because I'm paying attention to it," you could say, "That's right. You can continue to have that conflict, or you can attend to something else, as you continue to go deeper into trance and as that hand lifts up." So link it, and include it into their trance.

AUDIENCE: How about asking them if there is anything you can do for that?

That's a nice thing. "Is there anything that I could say to facilitate your experience, or is there anything to do right now?" That's perfect. Good addition, I like that. So do the exercise **now**.

(*The participants do the exercise.*)

Great! I was observing lots of trances and levitations.

EIGHT

I'm Only a Hypnotist, So
This Is Only a Suggestion

W E CAME TOGETHER TO LEARN solution-oriented hypnosis.
And I made you an outrageous claim at the beginning
of this, that by the end of this time you'd be able to induce a
trance. Yesterday, we spent all day working on induction and
how to do that. Today, we worked on what you do once they
get into trance, and how you get them to have specific experiences.
By now your unconscious mind is starting to get smart about playing tennis. That is, it's starting to get smart about doing trance.
Also, you had a good coach in that person who was sitting across
from you. Regardless of all the theories that you know and all the
books that you read, your clients are going to supervise you the
best.

I can tell you a story to send you off and make it more likely
that you put this stuff into practice. I learned something about
learning a while ago. I work at a place called the Hudson Center,
which is run by my wife, Pat [Hudson]. We have about a dozen
people working there, very able clinicians, people that have been
in the field for a long time. Our staff members have usually worked
other places and graduate into private practice after a while. So
we have people with a lot of experience. Occasionally, we have
somebody come on that doesn't have that much experience, but

rarely. A few years ago we had that situation. A student came through and did her internship there. Her name was Audrey Berlin. After she finished her internship, we invited her to join the staff as part-time administrator director and part-time clinician. After about six months I noticed that in staff meetings she was talking about stuff that she was doing that had taken me six years to learn. How did Audrey Berlin learn this stuff in six months when it took me six years, I wondered. She was getting hand and arm levitations, automatic handwriting, amnesias, and anesthesias. She was doing brief therapy stuff and solution-oriented stuff.

Now I knew they didn't teach her this stuff in her graduate program. So I watched her for a while and came to the realization that there was an Audrey Berlin learning style, which was very different from the Bill O'Hanlon learning style. The Bill O'Hanlon learning style is to go to a workshop, read a book, think about it a lot, go to another workshop, read another book, get enthusiastic, and buy a bunch more books. Then, get so busy you don't have time to read the books, so go to another workshop to figure out what was in those books you should have been reading. Then go to another workshop, think about it some more, obsess about it, talk to your friends about it, think you're gonna try it, but you know you don't know enough yet so you go to another workshop, or read another book or article or think about it for a lot longer, than finally you try it. That's the Bill O'Hanlon style of learning.

The Audrey Berlin style of learning is: Go to a workshop on Saturday and Sunday, and on Monday go back to your practice and try it out. You either say to your clients, "Hey, I went to this workshop this weekend, I don't really know what I'm doing yet, but how about if we try it?" Pick some client you like and trust. Or you just go in and try it. She would read an article and, in the next session, she would try it. And I thought, "What an innovative learning approach, I *never* thought of that." I would have never even considered it.

Once I learned the Audrey Berlin way of doing things, I decided that I would take up the Audrey Berlin way of learning things. That means that the Bill O'Hanlon way of learning things is available for rent or lease or purchase for anybody who would particularly like to use it. But, of course, I'd recommend you use the Audrey Berlin method. I'm only a hypnotist, so this is only a suggestion.

The other thing that I might suggest is that there have been a lot of things happening here this weekend. A lot of information has been coming at you both consciously and unconsciously through a lot of different modalities. Through the handouts, videos, audios, through demonstrations, through practice exercises, through talk, in the breaks, and during lunch. It will probably take a little while for all that to percolate down and bubble up and for you to figure out what's useful for you and what's not useful for you. So I'd say that probably what's best at this point is to just let it all sort of soak down at the unconscious level and then, when you have a chance to, go practice it. Meanwhile, let it percolate down and let yourself just relax, and enjoy the rest of the evening and feel refreshed.

Some of you have been working very hard, and I would say, "Just let it go," and let yourself complete this workshop in a way that really works for you. Integrate things at the conscious and unconscious level, feel free to ignore or tune out whatever I've said that hasn't really been appropriate for you or hasn't really contributed to you. Feel free to take some of the things I say and translate them into your own understanding so that you can really take this stuff and make it your own. Again, that's a suggestion. It's only a suggestion, and it's up to you to do that.

What I really want to say also, just to complete, is that I've really, you might have noticed, had a great time teaching this workshop. I'm very passionate about these hypnotic and solution-oriented ideas. I really appreciate you being here, thank you for showing up and allowing me to do what it is that I really enjoy. I'm so passionate about these ideas because I think they empower people. I think if we can empower people and help people, maybe we can make this world work a bit better. So if you really enjoyed the workshop, what I'd like you to do is go out and contribute to people and empower people. Maybe if you can do that, maybe we can have a world that works. One in which we don't blow each other up and that has a little peace and where people who don't get abused. That shouldn't happen. And people shouldn't starve to death or not have homes. Maybe we can do a little perestroika in our country and see if we can make things work a little better here.

This is one of my ways to contribute to other people, so if you were moved and touched by the workshop, please go out and move and touch other people. Thank you for being here.

THUNDEROUS APPLAUSE

ERICKSONIAN BIBLIOGRAPHY

Primary Sources

Cooper, Linn, & Erickson, Milton H. *Time Distortion in Hypnosis* (Reissued). New York: Irvington, 1982.

Erickson, Milton H., Hershman, Seymour, & Secter, Irving I. *The Practical Application of Medical and Dental Hypnosis* (Reissued). Chicago: Seminars on Hypnosis Publishing Co., 1981.

Erickson, Milton H., Rossi, Ernest L., & Rossi, Sheila I. *Hypnotic Realities: The Induction of Clinical Hypnosis and Forms of Indirect Suggestion.* New York: Irvington, 1976.

Erickson, Milton H., & Rossi, Ernest L. *Hypnotherapy: An Exploratory Casebook.* New York: Irvington, 1979.

Erickson, Milton H., & Rossi, Ernest L. *Experiencing Hypnosis: Therapeutic Approaches to Altered States.* New York: Irvington, 1981.

Erickson, Milton H., & Rossi, Ernest L. *The February Man: Evolving Consciousness and Identity in Hypnotherapy.* New York: Brunner/ Mazel, 1989.

Haley, Jay. *Advanced Techniques of Hypnosis and Therapy: Selected Papers of Milton H. Erickson, M.D.* New York: Grune & Stratton, 1967.

Haley, Jay. *Conversations with Milton H. Erickson, M.D. Volume I: Changing Individuals; Volume II: Changing Couples; Volume III: Changing Children and Families.* New York: Triangle (Norton), 1985.

Havens, Ronald. *The Wisdom of Milton H. Erickson.* New York: Irvington, 1984.

O'Hanlon, William H., & Hexum, Angela L. *An Uncommon Casebook: The Complete Clinical Work of Milton H. Erickson.* New York: Norton, 1990.

195

Rosen, Sidney. *My Voice Will Go With You: The Teaching Tales of Milton H. Erickson*. New York: Norton, 1982.

Rossi, Ernest L. *The Collected papers of Milton Erickson on Hypnosis*. New York: Irvington, 1980.

Rossi, Ernest L., Ryan, Margaret O., & Sharp, Florence A. *Healing in Hypnosis: The Seminars, Workshops and Lectures of Milton H. Erickson, Volume I*. New York: Irvington, 1983.

Rossi, Ernest L., & Ryan, Margaret O. *Life Reframing in Hypnosis: The Seminars, Workshops and Lectures of Milton H. Erickson, Volume II*. New York: Irvington, 1985.

Rossi, Ernest L., & Ryan, Margaret O. *Mind-Body Communication in Hypnosis: The Seminars, Workshops and Lectures of Milton H. Erickson, Volume III*. New York: Irvington, 1986.

Rossi, Ernest L., & Ryan, Margaret O. *Creative Choice in Hypnosis: The Seminars, Workshops and Lectures of Milton H. Erickson, Volume IV*. New York: Irvington, 1992.

Zeig, Jeffrey K. *A Teaching Seminar With Milton H. Erickson*. New York: Brunner/Mazel, 1980.

Zeig, Jeffrey K. *Experiencing Erickson: An Introduction to the Man and His Work*. New York: Brunner/Mazel, 1985.

Secondary Sources

Bandler, Richard, & Grinder, John. *Patterns of the Hypnotic Techniques of Milton H. Erickson, M.D. Volume I*. Cupertino, CA: Meta, 1975.

Combs, Gene, & Freedman, Jill. *Symbol, Story, and Ceremony: Using Metaphor in Individual and Family Therapy*. New York: Norton, 1990.

Dolan, Yvonne. *A Path with a Heart: Ericksonian Utilization with Resistant and Chronic Patients*. New York: Brunner/Mazel, 1985.

Dolan, Yvonne. *Resolving Sexual Abuse: Solution-Focused Therapy and Ericksonian Hypnosis for Adult Survivors*. New York: Norton, 1991.

Gilligan, Stephen. *Therapeutic Trances: The Cooperation Principle in Ericksonian Hypnotherapy*. New York: Brunner/Mazel, 1987.

Gordon, David, & Myers-Anderson, Maribeth. *Phoenix: Therapeutic Patterns of Milton H. Erickson*. Cupertino, CA: Meta, 1981.

Grinder, John, DeLozier, Judith, & Bandler, Richard. *Patterns of the Hypnotic Techniques of Milton H. Erickson, M.D. Volume 2*. Cupertino, CA: Meta, 1977.

Haley, Jay. *Uncommon Therapy: The Psychiatric Techniques of Milton H. Erickson, M.D.* New York: Norton, 1973.

Haley, Jay. *Ordeal Therapy: Unusual Ways to Change Behavior*. San Francisco: Jossey-Bass, 1984.

Havens, Ronald, & Walters, Catherine. *Hypnotherapy Scripts: A Neo-Ericksonian Approach to Persuasive Healing.* New York: Brunner/Mazel, 1989.

Kershaw, Carol J. *The Couple's Hypnotic Dance: Creating Ericksonian Strategies in Marital Therapy.* New York: Brunner/Mazel, 1992.

Klippstein, Hildegard. *Ericksonian Hypnotherapeutic Group Inductions.* New York: Brunner/Mazel, 1991.

Lankton, Stephen, & Lankton, Carol. *The Answer Within: A Clinical Framework of Ericksonian Hypnotherapy.* New York: Brunner/Mazel, 1983.

Lankton, Stephen, & Lankton, Carol. *Enchantment and Intervention in Family Therapy: Training in Ericksonian Approaches.* New York: Brunner/Mazel, 1986.

Lankton, Stephen, & Lankton, Carol. *Tales of Enchantment: Goal-oriented Metaphors for Adults and Children in Therapy.* New York: Brunner/Mazel, 1989.

Lankton, Stephen (Ed.). *Elements and Dimensions of an Ericksonian Approach.* New York: Brunner/Mazel, 1985. [Ericksonian Monographs #1]

Lankton, Stephen (Ed.). *Central Themes and Principles of Ericksonian Therapy.* New York: Brunner/Mazel, 1987. [Ericksonian Monographs #2]

Lankton, Stephen, & Zeig, Jeffrey (Eds.). *Treatment of Special Populations with Ericksonian Approaches.* New York: Brunner/Mazel, 1988. [Ericksonian Monographs #3]

Lankton, Stephen, & Zeig, Jeffrey (Eds.). *Research, Comparisons and Medical Applications of Ericksonian Techniques.* New York: Brunner/Mazel, 1988. [Ericksonian Monographs #4]

Lankton, Stephen, & Zeig, Jeffrey (Eds.). *Ericksonian Hypnosis. Application, Preparation, and Research.* New York: Brunner/Mazel, 1989. [Ericksonian Monographs #5]

Lankton, Stephen, & Zeig, Jeffrey (Eds.). *Extrapolations: Demonstrations of Ericksonian Therapy.* New York: Brunner/Mazel, 1989. [Ericksonian Monographs #6]

Lankton, Stephen (Ed.). *The Broader Implications of Ericksonian Therapy.* New York: Brunner/Mazel, 1990. [Ericksonian Monographs #7]

Lankton, Stephen, Gilligan, Stephen, & Zeig, Jeffrey (Eds.). *Process and Action in Brief Ericksonian Therapy.* New York: Brunner/Mazel, 1991. [Ericksonian Monographs #8]

Leva, Richard (Ed.). *Psychotherapy; The Listening Voice: Rogers and Erickson.* Muncie, IN: Accelerated Development, 1988.

Lovern, John D. *Pathways to Reality: Erickson-Inspired Treatment Approaches to Chemical Dependency.* New York: Brunner/Mazel, 1991.

Mills, Joyce C., & Crowley, Richard J. *Therapeutic Metaphors for Children and the Child Within.* New York: Brunner/Mazel, 1986.

O'Hanlon, William Hudson. *Taproots: Underlying Principles of Milton Erickson's Therapy and Hypnosis.* New York: Norton, 1987.
Overholser, Lee C. *Ericksonian Hypnosis: Handbook of Clinical Practice.* New York: Irvington, 1984.
Ritterman, Michele. *Using Hypnosis in Family Therapy.* San Francisco: Jossey-Bass, 1983.
Zeig, Jeffrey K. (Ed.). *Ericksonian Approaches to Hypnosis and Psychotherapy.* New York: Brunner/Mazel, 1982.
Zeig, Jeffrey K. (Ed.). *Ericksonian Psychotherapy. Volume I: Structures; Volume II: Clinical Applications.* New York: Brunner/Mazel, 1985.
Zeig, Jeffrey K., & Lankton, Stephen R. (Eds.). *Developing Ericksonian Therapy: State of the Art.* New York: Brunner/Mazel, 1988.

Sources for Audio and Videotape Examples in the Text

Audiotape Example #1: Milton Erickson—Basic Induction. *Hypnotic Realities* (one cassette) from Irvington Publishers; accompanies the book *Hypnotic Realities.*

Audiotape Example #2: Milton Erickson—Induction with Permission and Splitting. *Life Reframing in Hypnosis* (one cassette) from Irvington Publishers; accompanies the book *Life Reframing in Hypnosis.*

Audiotape Example #3: Joseph Barber—Interspersal for Pain Control. *Introduction to Naturalistic Hypnosis* (one cassette) from Joseph Barber, 921 Westwood Blvd., Suite 201, Los Angeles, CA 90024.

Audiotape Example #4: Milton Erickson—Treatment of Tinnitus and Phantom Limb Pain. *Hypnotherapy* (one cassette) from Irvington Publishers; accompanies the book *Hypnotherapy.*

Videotape Example #1: Milton Erickson—Induction by Evocation. *1958 Milton H. Erickson Hypnotic Induction* (one videocassette) available from The Family Therapy Institute of Washington, DC, 5850A Hubbard Drive, Rockville, MD 20852.

Videotape Example #2: Milton Erickson—Hand/Arm Levitation (1958). *The Reverse Set in Hypnotic Induction* (one videocassette) available from Irvington Publishers.

Videotape Example #3: Bill O'Hanlon—Hypnotherapy for Sexual Abuse Aftereffects. Not available for sale or rent.

INDEX